Collins
English for Work

Workplace English 2
James Schofield

Collins

HarperCollins Publishers
77-85 Fulham Palace Road
Hammersmith
London W6 8JB

First edition 2012

Reprint 10 9 8 7 6 5 4 3 2 1 0

© HarperCollins Publishers 2012

ISBN 978-0-00-746055-7

Collins ® is a registered trademark
of HarperCollins Publishers Limited

www.collinselt.com

A catalogue record for this book is available
from the British Library.

Typeset in India by Aptara

Printed in China by Leo Paper Products Ltd.

Cameraman: Jamie Turner
Sound engineer: Stuart Thompson
Actors: David Shaw-Parker, Lucy Newman-Williams,
Piers Ronan, Davina Perera
Photographs by Toby Madden

Introduction

Welcome to Workplace English 2

This course gives you the English you need to work in teams on projects with colleagues and clients.

The 24 units are in four modules: 1–6, 7–11, 12–18, 19–24. For more information on the content and focus of the four modules read the information on page vi / vii.

Each unit begins with a conversation to watch or listen to, or an email to read. The conversations and emails present the key language. Then there is language analysis and activities for you to practise the key language including speaking exercises. There is an Answer key at the back of the book.

A DVD and Audio CD are included in the course. The DVD contains the video for Units 1 to 6 and 19 to 24.

If you see this symbol , you need to watch the DVD.

If you see this symbol , you need to listen to the audio CD.

We recommend you spend about 60 minutes on each unit.

In addition, at the back of the book there are very useful reference sections for you to use and refer to in your day-to-day work.

We hope you enjoy using this self-study course. Good luck in your business career!

Contents

The story

In *Workplace English 2* we follow Tom Field, a project manager at Lowis Engineering in London. Tom's current project is the integration of Lowis Engineering into Australian Power Utilities (APU). APU is based in Sydney. Lowis Engineering is in the process of being taken over by APU. In addition to the senior manager at Lowis Engineering responsible for the takeover negotiations (Diane Kennedy), Tom interacts with John Carter and Karen Taylor from APU.

Through the characters and story, you learn about the typical issues and problems that arise when two companies want and need to work closely together. This self-study pack shows how people on both sides can cooperate and find solutions. It looks at typical business situations such as meetings, presentations, telephoning, emailing and effective telephone and video conferencing.

Module 1

Units 1–6

These units take place at Lowis Engineering in London and focus on the first face-to-face meetings between Lowis Engineering and APU.

Module 2

Units 7–11

In these units, the characters are based in their own offices and we can follow the progress of the integration through emails, telephone calls and telephone conferences.

Module 3

Units 12-18

Again, the characters are working from their own offices and are communicating via email, phone and telephone conference to arrange a business trip to Sydney.

Module 4

Units 19–24

These units focus on a video conference meeting between London and Sydney to discuss the progress of the project.

Characters

Tom Field is a project manager at Lowis Engineering. He has a lot of business experience in managing change and is responsible for coordinating the integration of Lowis Engineering's computer systems with those of APU.

Diane Kennedy is a senior manager at Lowis Engineering. Tom reports to her and she is responsible for helping Tom deal with any difficulties that occur at Lowis Engineering with the integration work. She works mostly with her opposite number at APU, John Carter.

John Carter is the head of engineering and special projects at APU. He has to make sure that at a senior level the integration works and that if there are any problems, a solution is found.

Karen Taylor is the Chief Information Officer (CIO) at APU. She manages all the computer systems within APU and has to make sure that the systems from Lowis Engineering are able to work together with APU in the future.

1   Back in the office

Greeting colleagues ┃ Describing your weekend ┃ Explaining current activities

Conversation

01
DVD

1 Tom Field comes to work on Monday morning. Read the conversations and watch the video. What does his manager, Diane Kennedy, want him to do?

Tom	**Morning**, Cathy!
Cathy	**Morning**, Tom!
Tom	**Hi**, Julia!
Julia	**Hi**, Tom!
Diane	**Hello**, Tom. **How are you?**
Tom	**Hi, fine, thanks, and you?**
Diane	**Very well, thanks. Good weekend?**
Tom	Yeah, **great, thanks.** We had a children's birthday party for Emily yesterday and ten of her friends came round.
Diane	**Wow!**
Tom	**How was your weekend?**
Diane	**Very busy**, too. At the moment I'm working 24/7 on this APU takeover. So, is everything ready for the presentation today?
Tom	Yes, I think so. Jasmine is making photocopies of your presentation now and I'm just changing something on today's agenda, you know, the lunch at the restaurant.
Diane	Good.
Tom	Tom Field. Oh, hi. Right, OK, thanks! That was Cathy at reception. Jasmine is bringing John Carter and Karen Taylor up to the boardroom now.
Diane	All right! What are we waiting for? Let's go!

Business tip

1   When somebody greets you, you can repeat their greeting back to them:

Morning, Cathy!   *Good afternoon!*
Morning, Tom!   *Good afternoon!*

2   You can only ask about somebody's weekend on Monday. But on Friday you can ask about their plans for the weekend.

Understanding

01
DVD

2   **Watch again and answer the questions.**

   1   Does Tom know Cathy and Julia already?

   2   Did Tom enjoy his weekend?

   3   Who is making photocopies for Tom?

   4   What is Tom doing?

   5   Who telephones Tom?

   6   Where will Tom and Diane meet John Carter and Karen Taylor?

Key phrases

Greeting colleagues	Talking about your weekend
Morning!	*Good weekend?*
Hi!	*Great, thanks!*
Hello, … . How are you?	*How was your weekend?*
Fine, thanks, and you?	*Very busy!*
Very well!	

Practice

3   **Join the two parts of the sentences together.**

1	Hello,	**A**	and you?
2	How was	**B**	are you?
3	Very	**C**	Jasmine!
4	How	**D**	busy!
5	Fine thanks,	**E**	your weekend?

4 Complete the exchanges. Use the Key phrases and the Business tip boxes to help you.

1 A: _____!   B: Hello!

2 A: _____?   B: Great, thanks!

3 A: _____?   B: Very busy, especially Sunday.

4 A: Good morning!   B: _____!

5 A: _____?   B: Fine thanks, and you?

01 CD

5 Tom is talking to another colleague, Roberta. Put the sentences into the correct order to make a conversation. Then listen to Track 01 to check.

1	Tom	Morning, Roberta.
	Roberta	Great, thanks. I played golf on Sunday. How was your weekend?
	Tom	Fine, thanks. Good weekend?
	Tom	Very nice, thanks.
	Roberta	Morning, Tom. How are you?

Language spotlight

The present continuous for current activities

I'm working 24/7.
Jasmine is making some photocopies.
I'm just changing the agenda.
What are we waiting for?

We use the present continuous to talk about things that are happening around us now.

Go to page 118 for more information and practice.

Speaking

6 When you are greeting a colleague, it is important to sound enthusiastic and pleased to see them. Listen to Track 02 and repeat the phrases and questions.

02
CD

1 Morning, Cindy!

2 How are you?

3 Fine thanks, and you?

4 Very well!

5 How was your weekend?

6 Great, thanks!

7 It's Monday morning in the office and Colin, a colleague of yours, is just back from vacation. Read through the prompts and responses before you press play. Play Track 03 and speak after the beep. Then listen to Track 04 to compare your conversation.

03–04
CD

Colin	Morning!
You	*(Reply.)*
Colin	How are you?
You	*(Say you're fine and ask about him.)*
Colin	Very well, thanks. Good vacation?
You	*(Reply and ask about his vacation.)*
Colin	Very good, thanks. We went to France. What are you working on at the moment?
You	*(Say you're practising your English.)*
Colin	That's a good idea!
You	*(Ask Colin what he's doing.)*
Colin	Oh, I'm waiting for some coffee.

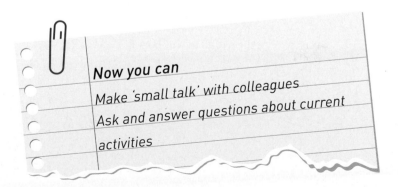

Now you can

Make 'small talk' with colleagues

Ask and answer questions about current activities

2 Visitors to the company

Welcoming company guests | Exchanging business cards | Describing your job

Conversation

02
DVD

1 Diane Kennedy and Tom Field from Lowis Engineering meet John Carter and Karen Taylor from APU. Read their conversation and watch the video. Who has Diane never met?

Diane	Hello, John! **Good to see you again!**
John	Diane! **Good to see you again, too. Can I introduce you to** Karen Taylor? She's Chief Information Officer at APU.
Diane	**Nice to meet you.**
Karen	**Nice to meet you, too,** Ms Kennedy.
Diane	**Please, call me** Diane. And **let me introduce** you to my colleague, Tom Field. Tom, John is head of engineering and special projects for APU.
Tom	**Pleased to meet you both. Let me give you my card.**
Karen	**Pleased to meet you, too** ... and **here's my card** ...
John	...and mine. So, **what do you do,** Tom?
Tom	Well, I work with Diane a lot! I'm a project manager. I'm responsible for some of the larger projects here at Lowis. And I'm also a change management specialist.
Karen	I see. So do you know many of the different department managers at Lowis?
Tom	I think so, yes. It's important to know the different people and their responsibilities here.
John	Oh yes, that's very important for a project manager.
Diane	Please, have a seat.

Business tip

People in companies often shorten job titles like this:

CEO = Chief Executive Officer, the person who manages the company.
CFO = Chief Financial Officer, the person who is in charge of the finances.
CIO = Chief Information Officer, the person who is in charge of the company's computer hardware and software.

When you speak to visitors, don't shorten job titles because they may not understand them. Always give the full job title.

Understanding

02
DVD

2 Watch again and choose the best answer for each question.

1 John has never met
  A Tom.
  B Karen.
  C Diane.

2 Karen Taylor works for
  A a Chief Information Officer.
  B Lowis Engineering.
  C APU.

3 Tom is in charge of
  A Lowis Engineering.
  B large projects in Lowis Engineering.
  C specialists in Lowis Engineering.

Key phrases

Welcoming company guests and exchanging business cards

Good to see you again!	Let me introduce ... .
Good to see you again, too.	Pleased to meet you both.
Can I introduce you to ... ?	Pleased to meet you, too.
Nice to meet you.	Let me give you my card.
Nice to meet you, too.	Here's my card.
Please, call me	What do you do?

Practice

3 Match the sentences.

1 Can I introduce you to Tom?
2 Let me give you my card.
3 What do you do?
4 Nice to meet you, Mr Martinez.
5 Good to see you!

A I'm a computer specialist.
B Good to see you, too.
C Please, call me Carlos.
D Thanks. Here's mine.
E Nice to meet you.

4 Complete the sentences with these words.

at	for	in	of	to	to	too

1 Pleased _____ meet you, _____.
2 Diane is head _____ personnel _____ Lowis Engineering.
3 I'm responsible _____ the company finances.
4 Can I introduce you _____ Robert?
5 She's a specialist _____ Java programming.

05
CD

5 Use the words to complete the sentences in the conversation. Then listen to Track 05 to check your answers.

Jasmine   Hi, John / good / see / again /

_____ .

John   Hello, Jasmine / good / see / again / too /

_____ .

Jasmine   Can / introduce / colleague / Julia /

_____ .

John   Pleased / meet / you /

_____ .

Julia   Pleased / meet / too /

_____ .

John   What / do, Julia /

_____ ?

Julia   I / Mr Fisher's / personal assistant /

_____ .

Language spotlight

The present simple tense for regular activities

She's Chief Information Officer.
What do you do?
I'm responsible for ... .

We use the present simple tense to talk about things that we always do.

Go to page 119 for more information and practice.

Speaking

 6 Notice how the underlined words are stressed in the exchanges below.
06 Listen to Track 06 and repeat the sentences.

1 <u>Good</u> to see you again!

Good to see you again <u>too</u>.

2 <u>Pleased</u> to meet you both.

Pleased to meet you <u>too</u>.

3 <u>Nice</u> to meet you.

Nice to meet you <u>too.</u>

 7 With a colleague, Tom, you are visiting Jenny, a supplier to your
07–08 company who you already know. Read through the prompts and
CD responses before you press play. Play Track 07 and speak after the
beep. Then listen to Track 08 to compare your conversation.

You	*(Greet Jenny.)*
Jenny	Oh, hello! Good to see you again too! Can I introduce my colleague, Alex?
You	*(Greet Alex.)*
Alex	Nice to meet you too.
You	*(Ask what Alex does.)*
Alex	Oh, I'm responsible for sales and marketing. What about you?
You	*(Tell him your job.)*
Alex	Interesting.
You	*(Introduce your colleague, Tom, to Jenny and Alex.)*
Jenny, Alex, Tom	Hi ... hello ... pleased to meet you both.
You	*(Offer Alex your business card.)*
Alex	Oh, thanks. Here's mine!

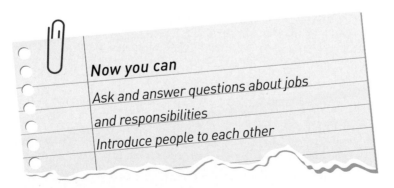

Now you can

Ask and answer questions about jobs

and responsibilities

Introduce people to each other

3   Down to business

Starting a meeting | Making requests | Talking about future plans

Conversation

03
DVD

1   Diane Kennedy and Tom Field from Lowis Engineering are meeting John Carter and Karen Taylor from APU to discuss the takeover of Lowis by APU. Read their conversation and watch the video. Who is Tom going to help?

Diane	**So, thank you**, everybody, **for coming to this meeting** today. **Let's start by** discussing what we're going to do over the next few months. John and Karen, you are going to be responsible from the APU side for integrating Lowis into APU.
John	That's right. I'm going to deal with the management side with you and Karen is going to work on systems like IT.
Diane	And **Tom, I want you to** work with Karen.
Tom	OK. How I can help exactly?
Karen	Well, **I'd like you to** help me understand how Lowis works. You're the expert. It's going to be difficult for me to integrate your system into APU without your support.
Tom	That's true.
Diane	Good. I think you're going to find this a very interesting project, Tom.
John	**We really need you to** make this work well, Tom.
Diane	Exactly. Let's look at the current situation at Lowis. Tom, **could you** give John and Karen the handouts while I start the projector?
John	**Would you mind if I** make a quick phone call while you set up?
Diane	Not at all.

Business tip

Particularly in English-speaking countries, it is usual for business people to use first names, even with people they meet for the first time.

John and *Karen*, *you're going to be responsible for... .*
We really need you to make this work well, *Tom*.

When you are in international meetings, listen and follow what other people do. If they use first names, you use first names.

Understanding

03
DVD

2 Watch again. Are the sentences true (T) or false (F)?

1 John and Karen are in charge of integrating Lowis into APU. T / F
2 Karen deals with HR issues for APU. T / F
3 Tom knows a lot about APU. T / F
4 Karen doesn't want Tom's help. T / F
5 Diane asks Tom to help her. T / F
6 John doesn't want to make a phone call. T / F

Key phrases

Starting meetings and making requests

Thank you for coming to this meeting.	*We really need you to ... .*
Let's start by ... +ing	*Could you ...?*
I want you to	*Would you mind if I ...?*
I would / I'd like you to ...	

Practice

3 Complete the sentences with language from Key phrases.

1 APU _____ like you to start work next week.
2 Would your boss _____ if I change our appointment?
3 I really _____ you to do this for me.
4 Thanks for _____ to this meeting.
5 _____ you send me an email?
6 Let's start _____ talking about the new project.

4 Put the words in the sentences into the correct order.

1 you / windows / mind / Would / we / open / if / the

_____ ?

2 boss / needs / him / really / call / you / to / The / give / a

_____ .

3 checking / start / information / by / some / Let's

_____ .

4 like / to / to / you / come / She'd / meeting / the

_____ .

5 reservation / check / you / Could / my

_____ ?

6 you / for / this / all / coming / morning / to / this / Thank / meeting

_____ .

5 You want a colleague at work, James, to do some things for you. Complete the requests with some information of your own.

1 James, I want you to ...

_____ .

2 Would you mind if I ...

_____ ?

3 Could you ...

_____ ?

4 The company really needs you to ...

_____ .

5 When that's finished, I'd like you to ...

_____ .

Language spotlight

Going to future

I'm going to deal with the management side.
It's going to be difficult for me to integrate your systems.
You're going to find this an interesting project.

The *going to* future is used to talk about future plans, intentions or expectations.

Go to page 121 for more information and practice.

Speaking

6 The two words *going to* are often run together when spoken quickly so that it sounds like *gonna*. Listen to Track 09 and repeat the sentences.

09
CD

1 I'm <u>going to</u> phone him.

2 He's <u>going to</u> send an email.

3 What are you <u>going to</u> do?

4 It isn't <u>going to</u> work.

5 Are you <u>going to</u> see him tomorrow?

7 You are a project manager. Ask the project team members to do things for you. Read through the prompts and responses before you press play. Play Track 10 and speak after the beep. You start. Then listen to Track 11 to compare your conversation.

10–11
CD

You	*(Thank Helen and Colin for coming to the meeting.)*
Helen + Colin	OK, good.
You	*(Ask Helen and Colin to do some things for you.)*
Helen + Colin	Fine. No problem.
You	*(Ask Colin to check the project costs.)*
Colin	Sure. Can I get the figures from you tomorrow morning?
You	*(Say you aren't going to be in the office tomorrow morning. Ask if he can come to your office after the meeting.)*
Colin	Of course.
You	*(Say you'd like Helen to check the factory with you.)*
Helen	Great! When?
You	*(Say you plan to check it on Monday next week.)*
Helen	OK.
You	*(Ask the team to send you all their reports to you by Friday lunch time.)*
Helen + Colin	Sure. No problem.

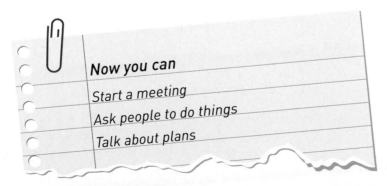

Now you can

Start a meeting

Ask people to do things

Talk about plans

4 The presentation

Starting a presentation | Sequencing a presentation | Talking about the past

Conversation

04
DVD

1 Diane and Tom are giving a presentation to John and Karen about Lowis. Read their conversation and watch the video. In which countries does Lowis have offices?

Diane	OK. So Tom and I **would like to tell you something about** the two biggest projects at Lowis over the last three years: **first**, there's the accounting software - xRoot - that we use for all of our bookkeeping, and **second**, the Jupiter project for the government. **So, first of all**, xRoot. Some years ago we used a basic spreadsheet for all of our bookkeeping. This wasn't a problem **then** because we worked in one London office. But **after** we opened offices in Strasbourg, Seoul and then Houston, we realized we needed to upgrade. The system was a problem at first, but we used some consultants to help us and now everything works very well.
Karen	Sorry, do you store your numbers in a Delphic or a Compex database?
Tom	Compex. xRoot only works with Compex.
Diane	Thanks, Tom.
Karen	I see.
Diane	So, **next** topic, Tom can tell you about the Jupiter project.
Tom	Thanks, Diane. Well, I was the project manager for the Jupiter project, which was a £45 ...

Business tip

It is a good idea to keep the structure of your presentations simple. This three-step approach works well:

1 Introduction: Tell the audience what your presentation is about.
2 Main body: Give the audience your points. Support each point with facts and figures.
3 Conclusion: Tell your audience what they need to do with the information you have given them.

Understanding

04 DVD

2 Watch the video again and choose the best answer for each question.

1 In her presentation Diane wants to talk about
   A Lowis offices around the world.
   B APU.
   C two large projects at Lowis.

2 The xRoot system
   A deals with financial figures.
   B deals with sales.
   C deals with office systems.

3 Tom
   A was project manager at xRoot.
   B was the project manager on the Jupiter project.
   C worked for the government.

Key phrases

Giving a presentation	Talking about the past
I would like / I'd like to tell you something about	*After ... , we did ... .* *Then ... .*
First, ... / First of all, ...	
Second, ...	
Third, ...	
Next	
Finally, ...	

3 Join the two parts of the sentences together.

1 We would like to	**A** look at these figures.
2 So, first of all,	**B** the project in Turkey, we then … .
3 After we finished	**C** six months in Indonesia with … .
4 Then we worked for	**D** show you our new product.

4 Complete the beginning of a presentation about APU with words from the Key phrases.

I would (1) _____ to tell you something about APU: (2) _____, our projects in Southeast Asia, (3) _____, our merger with Lowis Engineering and, thirdly, the Sydney traffic projects.

So, first of (4) _____, Southeast Asia. In 2005 we opened our offices in Jakarta, and Kuala Lumpur in 2007. (5) _____ we started working there, we realized how important it was to have local experts in our team and so we (6) _____ hired graduates from the local universities.

5 Complete a presentation about your company with some facts of your own.

1 I would like to tell you something about _____ .

2 Firstly, _____ .

3 Secondly, _____ .

4 So, first of all, _____ .

5 After we _____, we then _____ .

Language spotlight

The past simple

Some years ago we used Microsoft Excel … .
… we worked in one London office … .
This wasn't a problem then.
I was a project manager … .
… after we opened offices in Strasbourg … .

The past simple is used to talk about activities in the past that are finished.

Go to page 122 for more information and practice.

Speaking

🔊 **6** In presentations we usually pause after signal words like *first* and
12   *second* so that the audience knows something important is coming.
CD   Listen to Track 12 and repeat the phrases:

    1 First, the costs.

    2 Second, the size.

    3 So, first of all, the new plans.

    4 After that, we closed the company in Ankara.

    5 Then we opened a factory in Malaysia.

🔊 **7** You are giving a presentation to a group of suppliers. Use the notes to
13   write your presentation. Then listen to Track 13 to compare your
CD   presentation.

Notes

Topic: Payment terms

Want to talk about (1) change in terms (2) reasons for change in terms

Plan: payment terms to change from 60 to 90 days on January 1st.

Reason for change: 90 days is what our customers require.

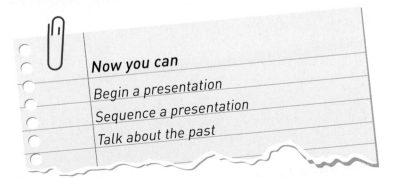

Now you can

Begin a presentation

Sequence a presentation

Talk about the past

5 Questions and answers at the presentation

Handling questions | Asking questions about the past

1 At the end of Diane and Tom's presentation John and Karen have some questions about Lowis. Read their conversation and watch the video. What was Diane responsible for in Seoul?

05 DVD

Tom	OK, so **do you have any questions?**
John	Yes. Diane, have you always worked here in London?
Diane	**Sorry, I don't understand your question.**
John	Well, I mean did you ever work at any of the Lowis offices outside Britain?
Diane	Ah, I see. **I'm glad you asked that question,** John. Yes, I did. In 2008 I was sales manager responsible for Asia and I worked in Seoul. But I didn't work there for very long, only about six months.
Karen	Were you responsible for the xRoot project in Asia?
Diane	No, I wasn't. That was my boss, Mr Lee Ji-Sung.
John	Ah yes, Mr Lee. I met him last week in Sydney. And how much did the new system cost?
Diane	**That's a good question** ... erm ... **I'm not sure about that**. Tom, do you know?
Tom	Yes. Including the Compex consultants it cost around six million dollars.
Karen	And how long did it take to install?
Tom	That was very fast. The project took nine months.
John	That is fast! **Now I have a question for you, Tom:** when did your work for the Jupiter project start?
Tom:	Oh, **let me think.** It began about 12 months ago when I started work on the ...

Business tip

Be positive about questions at the end of your presentation. It is a good chance to repeat key information or to give your listeners more information about your topic.

Understanding

05
DVD

2 Watch the video again. Are the sentences true (T) or false (F)?

1 Diane has only worked in London.   T / F
2 Diane worked for a short time in Seoul.   T / F
3 Diane's boss wasn't responsible for the xRoot project in Asia.   T / F
4 Tom says the xRoot project cost about six million dollars.   T / F
5 John doesn't think the xRoot project was fast.   T / F

Key phrases

Questions and answers at a presentation

Do you have any questions?	*I'm not sure about that.*
Sorry, I don't understand your question.	*[Now] I have a question for you, Tom.*
I'm glad you asked that question.	*Let me think.*
That's a good question.	

Practice

3 Look at the sentences below and write in the missing word.

1 I'm you asked that question. _____
2 Sorry, I don't your question. _____
3 That's a question! _____
4 Have a question for you, Kim. _____
5 Let think. _____

4 Put the words in the sentences into the correct order.

1 Do / presentation / you / the / any / questions / have / about

_____?

2 not / sure / I'm / about / that / point

_____.

3 question / me / think / Let / about / that

_____.

4 you / question / for / asking / Thank / that

_____.

5 What do you say when:

1 you want people to ask you questions after your presentation?

_____

2 you don't understand a question?

_____

3 you aren't sure of the answer to a question?

_____

4 you want some time to think about the answer to a question?

_____

Language spotlight

The past simple: questions and negatives

Were you responsible for the xRoot project?
Did you ever work outside Britain?
I didn't work there long.
No, I wasn't.
How much did the new system cost?

Go to page 122 for more information and practice.

Speaking

6 When you ask questions, the intonation is very important so that people realize you are asking a question. Listen to Track 14 and repeat the questions.

14 CD

1 How much did it cost?
2 What did you do?
3 How long were you there?
4 Were you the sales manager?
5 When did you arrive?

7
15–16
CD

After you make a presentation, your customer wants to ask some questions about your new product. Use the information below to help you answer the questions. Read through the prompts and responses before you press play. Play Track 15 and speak after the beep. Then listen to Track 16 to compare your presentation.

You	*(Ask if there are questions.)*
Customer 1	Yes. How much time did you need to develop your product?
You	*(Say you don't understand.)*
Customer 1	I mean, how long did it take from start to finish?
You	*(Nine months.)*
Customer 2	Was the product tested in Taiwan?
You	*(Say you aren't certain. Ask if you can send an email with the answer.)*
Customer 2	Of course. How many people worked on the project?
You	*(Say you are glad he asked that question. Say it wasn't many, only six engineers.)*

 8
17–18
CD

Now take the part of the customer and ask more questions about the new product. Use the information below to help you ask the questions. Play Track 17 and speak after the beep. Then listen to Track 18 to compare.

You	*(Ask if the supplier was responsible for the project.)*
Supplier	Yes, I was.
You	*(Ask how much the project cost.)*
Supplier	I'm afraid I can't tell you that information.
You	*(Say you understand. Ask where the six engineers worked.)*
Supplier	They worked as a team in the UK.
You	*(Say thanks.)*
Supplier	My pleasure.

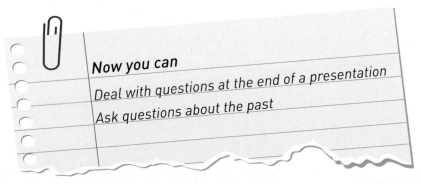

Now you can

Deal with questions at the end of a presentation

Ask questions about the past

6 Closing the meeting

Finishing a meeting I Setting objectives I Offering refreshments

Conversation

1 At the end of the meeting Diane makes a summary of the discussion. Read their conversation and watch the video. What does Tom promise Karen?

Diane	OK, **let me summarize**: Tom will work with Karen on the integration project full time. Karen will report to John and Tom will report to me.
John	Right, and you and I, Diane, we'll have a meeting or telephone call once a week to check progress.
Diane	Yes.
Tom	OK. So, Karen, I'll make a list of all the IT systems for you so that you know what we have.
Karen	Great! When will you be able to send that to me?
Tom	It'll be on your desk on Wednesday.
Diane	**Are you OK with that**, John?
John	Oh, yes. That's great.
Diane	Good ... Well, **I think that's enough for today**.
John	Good.
Diane	Ah, excellent timing. Now, you and I, John, have a factory tour with Chris Fox the production manager in half an hour and since we won't have time for a proper lunch, I ordered some sandwiches for us all.
John	Thank you.
Karen	Good idea.
Diane	So, **help yourself to something**.
Karen	Thank you.

John	Looks good.
Diane	Tom, **could you pass me a** bottle of water?
Karen	**Sorry, is that chicken? I'm afraid I don't eat meat.**
Tom	Oh, sorry. **Would you like some of these** sandwiches? Cheese, egg and ... I think those ones are salad sandwiches.
Karen	I think I'll just have some fruit, thanks.
Diane	Good idea. **Have some** of this mango. **It's delicious!**

Business tip

When you offer guests food or drink, be careful to check if they have any special requirements. They may not eat certain foods. If you can plan this, find out before the meal.

Understanding

06
DVD

2 Watch the video again and correct each of the sentences below.

1 Tom and Karen will work on the integration project part time. _____
2 John and Diane will have a meeting every month. _____
3 On Friday Tom will send the list of IT systems to Karen. _____
4 Diane ordered some pizzas for lunch. _____
5 Karen doesn't eat fruit. _____

Key phrases

1 Finishing a meeting

Let me summarize:	*I think that's enough for today.*
Are you OK with that?	

2 Refreshments

Help yourself to something.	*Would you like some ...?*
Could you pass me ... ?	*Have some ... .*
Sorry, is that chicken?	*It's delicious.*
I'm afraid I don't eat meat.	

Practice

3 **Join the two parts of the sentence together.**

1	Let me summarize	A	bottle of water?
2	Would you like a	B	OK with that?
3	Are you	C	our meeting.
4	I'm afraid	D	sandwiches.
5	Have some	E	I can't eat nuts.

4 **Make sentences using these words to help you.**

1 think / enough / today _____ .

2 Please / yourself / something / eat _____ .

3 Could / pass / orange juice / John? _____ ?

4 Would / like some / fruit _____ ?

5 **Write the first part of the dialogue for each answer below.**

1 A _____

 B A mineral water? Here you are!

2 A _____

 B Yes, that's fine for me and my company.

3 A _____

 B Some cheese? Oh yes, thanks very much.

4 A _____

 B No problem. We can order some vegetarian food.

5 A _____

 B Mmm, you're right! The mango is delicious!

Language spotlight

Will future

It'll be on your desk ... [promise]
We won't have time ... [prediction]
Tom will work with Karen. [instructions]
Karen will report to John. [instructions]
When will you be able to send ... ? [instructions]

Will is used when we promise or predict something, or when we want to give instructions.

Go to page 123 for more information and practice.

Speaking

6 When speaking, we usually contract *will*. Listen and repeat the examples.

19 CD

1 It'll cost a lot of money.
2 What'll he do?
3 She won't be at the meeting.
4 Tom'll finish the report tomorrow.
5 When'll he call her?
6 They'll fly back tomorrow.

7 At the end of your meeting, you offer your American colleague, Cindy, some refreshments. Use the information to help you have a conversation with her. Read through the prompts and responses before you press play. Play Track 20 and speak after the beep. Then listen to Track 21 to compare your presentation.

20–21 CD

You	*(Say that's the end of the meeting.)*
Cindy	That's good.
You	*(Say you ordered some refreshments. You hope Cindy is hungry!)*
Cindy	Yes. Very.
You	*(Tell her to help herself.)*
Cindy	Mmm, it looks great!
You	*(Ask her to pass you an orange juice.)*
Cindy	Here you are. Um … is that beef in the sandwich? I'm afraid I don't eat meat!
You	*(Offer her some cheese salad sandwiches.)*
Cindy	Oh thanks! Sorry to be difficult!
You	*(No problem. Tell her you can't eat fish.)*

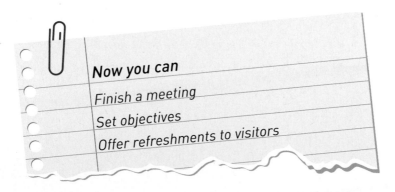

Now you can

Finish a meeting

Set objectives

Offer refreshments to visitors

7 On the phone to Australia

Telephoning a business partner | Asking for somebody on the phone

Telephone call

🔊 22 CD

1 Tom wants to speak to Karen in Australia. Listen to the telephone conversation. Why can't Tom speak to Karen in Sydney?

1	Kim	**Kim Benders speaking**.
	Tom	**Hello, this is** Tom Field **from** Lowis Engineering in London. **Can I speak to Karen Taylor, please?**
	Kim	Oh hello, Mr Field. I'm Karen's assistant. **I'm afraid she's not in the office** today. **She's on a business trip to** Malaysia. **Can I help you?**
	Tom	Oh, I see. Well, **can you put me through to** John Carter?
	Karen	Of course. **Hold the line, please**. Hello, Mr Field? **I'm sorry but his line's busy at the moment. Can I take a message**?
	Tom	No, don't worry. **I'll call him back later**.
	Kim	By the way, I know that Karen checks her emails every evening.
	Tom	Yes, that's a good idea. **I'll send her an email. Thanks for your help**.
	Kim	And she'll be back in the office on Friday, so you can speak to her then.
	Tom	OK. Good to know. Thanks a lot.
	Kim	No worries.
	Tim	Goodbye!
	Kim	Bye!

Business tip

Thanks for your help.
Always thank assistants when you speak to them. They will remember you as a pleasant business contact and be more willing to help you if you want to contact their manager in the future.

Understanding

**22
CD**

2 Listen again and choose the best answer for each question.

1 Kim Benders

   A works for Lowis Engineering.

   B is Karen's boss.

   C works for Karen.

2 John is

   A in Malaysia.

   B speaking on the phone.

   C in a meeting.

3 Tom wants

   A Kim to tell John to telephone him.

   B Kim to tell John he telephoned.

   C to telephone John later.

4 Tom decides to

   A write to Karen.

   B telephone Karen later.

   C visit Karen.

Key phrases

Telephoning

Calling a business partner	Answering the phone
Hello, this is Tom Field from … .	*Kim Benders speaking.*
Can I speak to Karen Taylor, please?	*I'm afraid she's not in the office.*
Can you put me through to … ?	*She's on a business trip to … .*
I'll call back later.	*Can I help you?*
I'll send her an email.	*Hold the line, please.*
Thanks for your help.	*I'm sorry but his line's busy at the moment.*
	Can I take a message?

Practice

3 Join the two parts of the sentences together.

1	Hold	**A**	take a message?
2	Can I	**B**	back later.
3	I'll call	**C**	for your help.
4	Thanks	**D**	speaking.
5	David Knopf	**E**	the line, please.

4 Put the words in the sentences into the correct order.

1 you / please / put / through / me / to / Can / Julia,

_____?

2 afraid / meeting / he's / I'm / in / a / at / moment / the

_____.

3 I / Jasmine / speak / Goodman, / to / Can / please

_____?

4 him / write / an / I'll / email

_____.

5 Knopf / this / xRoot / Software / is / David / Hi, / from

_____.

5 What do you say in these telephone situations?

1 The telephone rings and you answer.

_____

2 The caller wants to speak to your manager. She's in a meeting.

_____

3 You want the caller to wait while you transfer their call to somebody else.

_____

4 You have to tell the caller that the person they want is speaking on the phone.

_____

5 You offer to take a message.

_____

Language spotlight

Phrasal verbs

Well, can you **put** me **through** to John Carter?
I'll **call** him **back** later.

Go to page 124 for further information on phrasal verbs and practice.

Speaking

 6 When you want somebody to do something for you, add *please* at the
23
CD
end of the sentence. This will help you to get what you want! Listen and repeat the sentences below.

1 Can I speak to Karen Taylor, please?
2 Can you put me through to Susie Goh, please?
3 Can you take a message, please?
4 Hold the line, please.

7 You need to call your supplier, Compex Inc, in the US. Read through the
24–25
CD
prompts and responses before you press play. Play Track 24 and speak after the beep. Then listen to Track 25 to compare your conversation.

Jodie   Compex Incorporated, Jodie King speaking. How can I help you?
You   *(Give your name and your company name and ask to speak to Frank Linker.)*
Jodie   I'm afraid he's in a meeting.
You   *(Say you'll send him an email. Then ask to be put through to Susie Goh.)*
Jodie   I'm sorry but her line's busy at the moment. Can I take a message?
You   *(Tell her not to worry and you'll call back later. End the call politely.)*
Jodie   Goodbye!

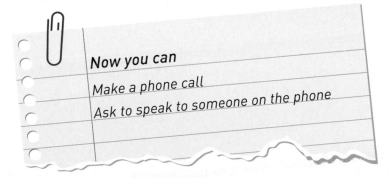

Now you can

Make a phone call

Ask to speak to someone on the phone

8   Emailing Australia

Making suggestions | Making an appointment | Creating an out-of-office message

Email

1   Tom sends an email to Karen. What does Tom suggest?

Dear Karen

I tried to call you today **but** I heard you are on a business trip.

With regard to your email and your questions, **I think it's a good idea if** we discuss them with Diane, John and some other people from Lowis. **I suggest that** I organize a telephone conference call on Friday at 8 am UK time (6 pm in Australia). Your assistant said you'll be back in the office then. **Could you let me know if that's convenient for you?**

I look forward to speaking to you soon.

Best wishes
Tom

I am out of the office until Thursday 7th November. I will be back in the office on Friday 8th November. I will be reading my emails every evening.

Thanks, Karen

Business tip

Dear Karen
Although there are different ways to start emails, starting with *Dear ...* is usually best for business emails. The alternatives, *Hello Karen, Hi Karen, Karen,* can sound too informal. Only use a first name if you know the person.

Understanding

2 Read the emails again. Are the sentences true (T) or false (F)?

1	Tom spoke to Karen.	T / F
2	Karen isn't on a business trip.	T / F
3	Diane wants to organize a telephone conference call.	T / F
4	Karen is back in the office on Thursday.	T / F
5	Karen is reading her emails on her business trip.	T / F

Key phrases

Business emails

1 Business emails	2 Making suggestions and appointments
I tried to call you ... but	
With regard to	*I think it's a good idea if ... .*
I look forward to speaking to you soon.	*I suggest that I ... .*
Best wishes	*Could you let me know if that's convenient for you?*

3 Automated replied	
I am out of the office [in ...] until	

Practice

3 Find the missing word for each sentence in the box.

a   but   me   until   we   your

1 With regard to project in India ....

_____

2 I think it's good idea if we ...

_____

3 I tried to speak to you this morning you were in a meeting.

_____

4 I suggest that meet as soon as possible.

_____

5 Could you let know if that's convenient?

_____

6 I'm out of the office Monday.

_____

4 **Put the sentences in this email to Diane's assistant, Jasmine Goodman, into the correct order.**

Dear Ms Goodman

_____ : Best wishes

_____ : With regard to our meeting tomorrow, ...

_____ : I look forward to seeing you tomorrow.

_____ : I suggest that I invite our accountant, Gordon King, to the meeting.

__1__ : I tried to call you this afternoon but you were in a meeting.

_____ : I think it's a good idea if we also discuss the project costs.

Priti Makesch

5 **You are writing an email to a business partner. Complete the email with information of your own.**

Dear _____

(1) _____ I tried to call you (2) _____ but
your assistant said you are (3) _____ .

With regard to your (4) _____ I think it's a good idea if I
(5) _____ . Also, I suggest that I (6) _____ .

Could you let me know if that's convenient for you?

Best wishes

(7) _____

Language spotlight

in / on / at prepositions of time

I suggest that I organize a telephone conference **on** *Friday* **at** *8 am.*
I will be back in the office **on** *Friday 8 th November.*
We use:
In for months and years: *In July / In 1989*
On for days of the week and dates: *On Friday / On May 30 th*
At for clock times and festivals: *At eight o'clock / At Christmas*

Go to page 125 for a full review of prepositions of time and a practice exercise.

Writing

6   An important US customer has left a message on your voice mail with several questions about your company's products or services. You tried to call her but she is flying to China. Send an email to say you want to speak to her and suggest you call her tomorrow at 6 pm Beijing time. Ask for her hotel telephone number.

7   Write an out-of-office reply for yourself for next week. You are going to be away all week on vacation and your assistant Susan Smith on smith@XYZ.com can deal with any enquiries.

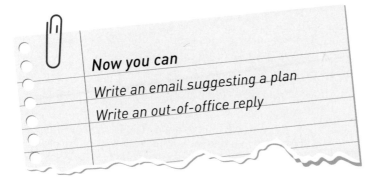

Now you can

Write an email suggesting a plan

Write an out-of-office reply

9 Starting the telephone conference call

Taking part in a telephone conference call (telco) | Greeting other participants

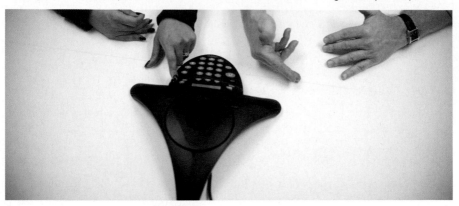

Telephone conference call

26
CD

1 Tom, Diane, John, Karen and Robert take part in a telco. Listen to the conversation. Where is Tom?

Recorded voice	**Welcome to the Maxtime telephone conference service. Please enter your conference call PIN followed by the pound sign. Please give your name.**
Tom	Tom Field.
Recorded voice	Until the other participants arrive, you will hear some music.
Recorded voice	**Another participant is entering the call.**
John	Hi, John Carter here. Hello, Tom?
Tom	Hi there.
John	**I'm sitting here with Karen.**
Karen	Morning, Tom.
Tom	Hello, Karen, hi John. **I'm not calling from the office** because **I'm working at home** today. But Diane **will call in in a minute**, together with Robert Holden. You want to ask him about the xRoot systems for the accounting department.
Recorded voice	Another participant is entering the call.
Diane	Hello. Diane and Robert here.
Robert	Hi, everybody. **Sorry we're late**.
Tom	No problem. **Well, let's start**. Karen, you have some questions for Robert and me, I think.
Karen	Yes, thanks Tom. Robert, **can you tell me** how many different IT systems you need for the financial accounts for Lowis?

Robert	Hmm, we use three systems.
Karen	Yes, but **why do you have** three IT systems?
Robert	Because Lowis is an international company. One system is for the local figures in each country – the US, Korea or Germany. The second system collects the figures from all over the world. The third system prepares the figures for our management and the tax office.
Karen	And how much time does the process need?
Robert	Not much. We can prepare the complete annual report in two days.
John	Yes, that is good. Tell me, Robert, **how many** people work in the accounts department?
Robert	Only a few. Including the trainees it's ... erm ... fifteen.
Karen	Right. Tom, can you tell me **how much** space the company computer servers need?
Tom	Only a little. We have them all in the basement. Maybe five square metres.
John	I see, Diane, what do you think about ... ?

Business tip

In a telco always listen carefully to the other speakers and let them finish what they have to say. Two people talking at the same time means nobody understands anything.

Understanding

26
CD

2 Listen again and answer the questions

1 Why is Tom not in the office?
2 Why does Lowis have three IT systems for the accounting department?
3 How long does it take to do the figures for Lowis?

Key phrases

Starting telcos	Asking questions
Tom here.	*Can you tell me ... ?*
I'm sitting here with Karen.	*Why do you have ... ?*
I'm calling from home.	*How much ... ?*
I'm working at home today.	*How many ... ?*
Diane will call in in a minute.	
Sorry we're late.	
Let's start.	

3 Join the two parts of the sentence together.

1	Sorry	A	computers do we need?
2	Let's	B	what you know about the software?
3	I'm working	C	start with the agenda.
4	Ken will call in	D	time do we need for the meeting?
5	Can you tell me	E	later.
6	How much	F	I'm late.
7	How many	G	from home today.

4 Put the words in the sentences into the correct order.

1 Mondays / home / Diane / from / on / works _____ .

2 sitting / Bernadette / here / with / I'm / Kim / and _____ .

3 you / costs / much / tell / Can / how / it / me _____ ?

4 you / many / know / worldwide / how / offices / you /
have / Do _____ ?

5 John and Karen have another telco with a Korean supplier, Mr Park.
Put the sentences into the correct order to make a conversation. Then
listen to Track 27 to check.

1	John	John Carter here. Hello, Mr Park.
	Mr Park	No problem, Ms Taylor.
	John	My colleague Karen Taylor will call in in a moment from home.
	John	Good. Well, let's start. Can you tell us how much time you have for us today?
	Karen	Hello, John. Hello, Mr Park. Sorry I'm late.
	Mr Park	As much time as you want, Mr Carter.
	John	Great! Well, first of all, we need to know how much your new products will cost?
	Mr Park	Good evening, Mr Carter.

Language spotlight

How much / How many / a little / a few

We use: *much* for things we cannot count (e.g. *How much space do we have?*), *many*
for things we can count (e.g. *How many computers do we have?*)
We answer *How much* with *a little* (e.g. *We only have a little space.*), We answer
How many with *a few* (e.g. *We only have a few computers.*)

Go to page 126 for further examples and a practice exercise.

Speaking

6 Practise the question forms. Listen and repeat the sentences.

28 CD

1 How much does it cost?
2 Can you tell me when she'll call in?
3 How many offices do you have?
4 Why do you have so many systems?

7 You are taking part in a telephone conference call with Jun Watanabe in Tokyo and Pascale Benoit in Paris to discuss a project you are working on together. Read through the prompts and responses before you press play. Play Track 29 and speak after the beep. Then listen to Track 30 to compare your conversation.

29–30 CD

Recorded voice	Another caller is entering the conference.
You	*(Say hello and give your name.)*
Jun + Pascale	Hi, Jun here. Hello, this is Pascale!
You	*(Apologize for being late.)*
Pascale	That's OK!
You	*(Say you're working from your home. Then ask how much time we need for the telco.)*
Jun	As much time as you want. Well, let's start. Can you tell us how many people you have for this project in your office?
You	*(Only a few. Ask Pascale how many people she has.)*
Pascale	Oh, it's the same for me. Only a few.
You	*(Ask Pascale how many people she needs.)*
Pascale	I think another five at least!

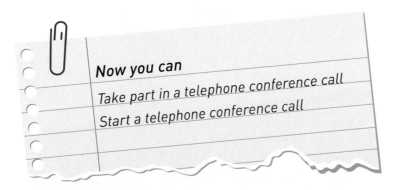

Now you can

Take part in a telephone conference call

Start a telephone conference call

10   Ending the telephone conference call

Making arrangements I Saying 'goodbye' on the phone I Talking about fixed plans

Telephone conference call

1   Tom, Diane, John, Karen and Robert are taking part in a telephone conference call. Listen to the conversation. How many nights is Tom staying in Portsmouth?

Diane	... and then we can integrate our computer system with yours and cut the number of computer servers.
Robert	And that cuts the costs, of course.
John	Yes, that's very important. Do you agree, Karen?
Karen	Yes, definitely. By the way Tom, **I just want to let you know** that I'm flying to London next week. Can we have a meeting some time? **What are your plans on** Monday?
Tom	**Let me check my schedule for next week**. Well, on Monday morning I'm having a meeting with the sales team to talk about your Customer Relationship Management tool.
Karen	**How does Monday afternoon look?**
Tom	Mm, **let me take a look**. Sorry, not good. After that, I'm driving down to Portsmouth to visit our largest customer and tell them about the company changes.
Karen	Well, can I come with you? Then I have a chance to see you and meet the customers of Lowis Engineering.
Tom	Well, I'm not sure if that's a good idea.
Diane	I think that's a really good idea, Tom. It's very important for Karen to meet our customers as soon as possible.
Tom	Yes, of course. It's just that I'm staying in Portsmouth on Monday night and I'm not driving back to London until Tuesday night.

Karen	No problem, Tom. I can take a train on Tuesday morning.
John	Excellent. That's a good solution, I think. Now, I have another meeting I'm afraid ...
Diane	Me too. **Good to speak to you**, John ... Karen.
Karen	Great! **Speak to you soon**, Diane and Robert. **Nice speaking to you**, Tom. See you on Monday
Tom	Right, Monday then. **I'm looking forward to it**, Karen.

Business tip

Great! Excellent!
You can use positive words like these to help improve your business relationships when your partner agrees with you about something.

Understanding

31
CD

2 Listen again. Are the sentences true (T) or false (F)?

1 Karen is flying to London tomorrow. T / F

2 Tom is busy all day on Monday. T / F

3 Tom is visiting a supplier in Portsmouth. T / F

4 Tom likes the idea of Karen going with him to Portsmouth. T / F

5 Karen will catch a train back to London on Tuesday. T / F

Key phrases

1 Making arrangements	2 Saying 'goodbye'
I just want to let you know	*Good to speak to you, ...*
What are your plans on ...?	*Speak to you soon.*
Let me check my schedule for next week.	*Nice speaking to you, ...*
How does Monday afternoon look?	*I'm looking forward to it.*
Let me take a look.	

Practice

3 Complete the sentences with one of these words.

lunchtime   Mr Carter's   seeing   speak   Tuesday

1 _____ to you soon.

2 How does Thursday _____ look?

3 Let me check _____ schedule for next week.

4 I'm looking forward to _____ you.

5 What are your plans on _____?

4 Match the sentences.

1	How does Saturday look?	**A**	Well, I'll go to work and finish the report.
2	What are your plans on Monday?	**B**	February? Let me check my calendar.
3	What about next month?	**C**	Yes, I think it should be a good meeting.
4	I'm looking forward to it!	**D**	Oh, I never do business on the weekend!

5 Read the conversation between John and a Korean supplier, Mr Park. In each numbered line there is at least one small mistake. Find and correct them.

1 J I just want to let you know. I'm flying to Seoul last week.

_____

2 P Oh, let my check me schedule.

_____

3 J How do Wednesday look?

_____

4 P Hmm, not too bad. What about on ten o'clock in your hotel?

_____

5 J That's fine. I'm have a meeting at the APU office after lunch.

_____

6 P OK. So, ten o'clock on Wednesday. Nice speaking at you, John.

_____

7 J Yes. He's looking forward to seeing you soon!

_____

Language spotlight

Present continuous to talk about the future

On Monday morning I'm having a meeting.
I'm staying in Portsmouth on Monday night.
I'm not driving back until Tuesday night.

We can use the present continuous to talk about things in the future which are already planned, organized and agreed.

Go to page 119 for further examples and practice.

Speaking

6 When you say goodbye to somebody on the phone it's important to
sound enthusiastic and friendly. If possible use the person's name.
Listen and repeat the sentences.

32
CD

1 Good to speak to you, Linda! Bye!

2 Speak to you soon, Kim!

3 Nice speaking to you, Ms Carter. Goodbye!

4 I'm looking forward to it, Pascale. Bye!

5 Well, goodbye then, Alex!

7 You are taking part in a telephone conference call with Jun Watanabe in
Tokyo to discuss a project you are working on together and to arrange a
meeting. Read through the prompts and responses before you press
play. Play Track 33 and speak after the beep. Then listen to Track 34 to
compare your conversation.

33–34
CD

Jun Well, I think a meeting is a very good idea.

You *(Say you are flying to Tokyo next week.)*

Jun Let me check the schedule.

You *(Ask about Tuesday afternoon.)*

Jun Oh, I'm sorry, I'm visiting a supplier outside Tokyo on Tuesday.

You *(Say you're staying in Tokyo until Friday.)*

Jun Oh, very good. Then I have a chance to see you on Thursday morning.

You *(Say you are meeting somebody at your hotel in the morning. Ask about his
plans for Thursday afternoon.)*

Jun Yes, that's fine. Is three o'clock OK?

You *(Say that's an excellent idea.)*

Jun Great. Well, it was good to speak to you, Karl. See you next week!

You *(Say you're looking forward to it and goodbye.)*

Jun Goodbye!

Now you can

Make arrangements

Talk about plans

11 Making plans by email

Making requests and suggestions | Talking about what is not allowed

Email

1 Karen sends an email to Tom. Read the email. What does she suggest?

Dear Tom

Following our telco discussion this afternoon, I had an idea. **Why don't I** come to your meeting on Monday morning with the Lowis sales team?

If this is OK for you, we can show your sales people the APU Customer Relationship Management system together. We must make sure they are happy about using it. Then **perhaps we could** all have lunch together before driving down to Portsmouth in the afternoon. **How do you feel about this?**

By the way, I'm going to take the train back to London on Monday night, after the meeting in Portsmouth. I have an appointment with Peter King from the Lowis legal department on Tuesday morning and I mustn't be late for that. John also says I have to check the servers in London as soon as possible. But I don't have to do anything else until Friday when I fly back to Sydney, so **shall we** meet again on Wednesday morning? If that's suitable for you, **do you think you could** reserve a meeting room in the office for us?

Best regards

Karen

Business tip

We must make sure ...
If you want your colleague to agree to do something it can help if you give them the feeling that you are doing something together by saying *we* instead of *you* or *I*.

Understanding

2 Read the email again. Find the mistake in each sentence and correct it.

1 John wants to come to Tom's meeting.
2 The salespeople already use the APU system.
3 Tom and Karen are taking the train to Portsmouth.
4 Karen must meet Diane Kennedy on Tuesday morning.
5 Karen mustn't check the servers for John.
6 Karen doesn't have to fly back to Sydney on Friday.

Key phrases

Making suggestions	Requests and asking for opinions
Why don't I ... ?	*How do you feel about this? / What's your opinion on ...?*
If this is OK for you, ...	
Perhaps we could	*Shall we ...?*
	Do you think you could ... ? / Would you mind + ing ... ?

Practice

3 Join the two parts of the sentence together.

1 How do you feel
2 What's your opinion
3 Shall we
4 Would you
5 Perhaps we

A mind booking me a flight?
B have a meeting next week?
C on this?
D could speak to Diane about this.
E about this issue?

4 Put the words in the sentences into the correct order.

1 to / you / and / mind / speaking / Jun / Would / Pascale

_____?

2 your / the / on / opinion / problem / What's

_____?

3 think / you / could / you / send / me / report / the / Do

_____?

4 send / the / the / figures / to / we / project / Shall / manager

_____?

5 this / for / is / OK / you / If, / we / work / together / can

_____ .

6 don't / meeting / have / we / a / on / Why / Wednesday

_____?

5 Complete the email below. Use the email on page 48.

Dear John

Following our meeting this morning, I spoke to my manager, Mr Lee.
I think it would be helpful if we had a telco to discuss your ideas.
(1) _____ I arrange a telco for next Friday morning? Perhaps
(2) _____ talk about the prices together.
How (3) _____ idea?

If (4) _____ you, we can also find a time for you to visit our
factory. You (5) _____ see how we make our motors, it's very
impressive!

Would (6) _____ emailing me to say if Friday is OK?
Many thanks

Best regards

Keow

Language spotlight

Modals for obligation

We <u>must</u> make sure = This is very important for me and 100% necessary.
I <u>mustn't</u> be late = It is very important for me that this does NOT happen.
John says I <u>have to</u> check = It is very important for somebody else that this happens.
I <u>don't have to</u> fly back to Sydney until Friday = It's not necessary.

Go to page 126 for further information and practice.

6 **You want to go to visit your colleague Pascale Benoit, in Paris. Write an email based on the notes below.**

- Say you are visiting Paris next week for a sales conference.
- Suggest you visit Pascale to discuss the project progress.
- Suggest you take her to lunch.
- Ask how she feels about this.
- Suggest you meet her at one o'clock at her office.
- Ask if she can make reservations in a restaurant.

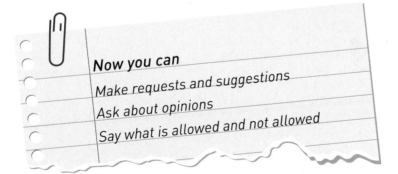

Now you can

Make requests and suggestions

Ask about opinions

Say what is allowed and not allowed

12 Telephone small talk

Making small talk on the phone | Making suggestions | Making arrangements

Telephone call

35
CD

1 John Carter calls Tom Field in London. Listen to their conversation. What is John's suggestion?

Tom	Tom Field.
John	Hi Tom, John here.
Tom	Well, good morning ... sorry, good afternoon, John. **How's the weather** there today?
John	Hot today and the radio says tomorrow will be hotter! My sons want me to take them down to the beach over the weekend so they can do a bit of surfing and we can have a barbecue.
Tom	**Sounds great! It's raining** here in London right now.
John	**Oh, too bad! Did you see** the football last night?
Tom	No, I missed it.
John	Good game. So **what's work like at the moment**?
Tom	Difficult! Not all the teams here are happy about the merger. And I think the legal department will be even more difficult. But Karen is going to talk to their boss, Peter King, soon.
John	Right. Umm. Tom, **I was wondering if you could** visit our offices here in Sydney? You could stay for a week and meet the people here.
Tom	Er ...well, yes, but have you spoken to Diane about it?
John	Not yet. She's not in the office at the moment. I'll call her again later.
Tom	I see. Well, ...
John	So, **when is a good time for you?**
Tom	Oh, well, **I have to check my schedule** first. I'll send an email with some suggestions. Is that OK?
John	Yes, that's fine and I have to speak to Diane. Good. Well, **what are you doing this weekend?** Are you doing anything ... ?

Business tip

How's the weather there today?
In many cultures it's a good idea to build up a friendly relationship with your business partners with small talk, even if you only meet on the phone. Small talk is general conversation about topics such as the weather, sport or work. It's important because people like to do business with people they like.

Understanding

35
CD

2 **Listen again and choose the best answer.**

1 Tom

   A has some problems with the merger.

   B doesn't have much work to do.

   C is going to a meeting.

2 John wants

   A to visit Lowis.

   B Tom to visit APU.

   C Tom to move to Sydney.

3 John

   A has written to Diane about Tom's proposed visit.

   B has spoken to Diane about Tom's proposed visit.

   C is going to speak to Diane about Tom's proposed visit.

Key phrases

1 Telephone small talk

How's the weather ... ?	*What are your plans for this weekend?*
What's work like at the moment?	*It's raining here.*
Did you see the football / tennis / basketball last night?	*Sounds great.*
	Too bad.
What are you doing this weekend?	

2 Making suggestions and arrangements

I was wondering if you could	*I have to check my schedule.*
When is a good time for you?	

Practice

3 **Complete the sentences with language from Key phrases.**

1 _____ your plans for next week?

2 _____ my schedule for Friday.

3 _____ see Pascale's presentation yesterday?

4 _____ could send me the figures.

5 _____ time for you to see me?

4 **Complete A's sentences.**

1 **A:** It's _____ .
   B: Really? It's raining here as well.

2 **A:** _____ you _____?
   B: For this evening? I'm going to the movies.

3 **A:** _____ at the moment?
   B: Terrible. We don't have enough people for all the work.

4 **A:** Did _____ last night?
   B: The football? No, I missed it.

5 **A:** _____? Thursday 2.00 pm?
   B: Thursday afternoon is great.

5 **Karen phones Peter King in the Lowis legal department to make an appointment. Put the sentences into the correct order to make a conversation. Then listen to Track 36 to check.**

36 CD

1	Karen	How's the weather in London?
	Peter	Hmm, I have to check my schedule. Oh, I'm sorry but the afternoon's no good.
	Peter	Well, on Tuesday perhaps.
	Karen	Sure. When's a good time for you? The afternoon, maybe?
	Peter	It's raining here.
	Karen	Well, what are you doing on Tuesday morning?
	Karen	Too bad! Listen, I'm visiting the UK next week. I was wondering if we could have a meeting some time?
	Peter	Tuesday morning is fine.

Language spotlight

Comparatives

Hot – hotter
Difficult – more difficult
The comparative is used to compare things or people that are different from each other. Short words, for example *hot*, add *er – hotter*. Longer words, for example *difficult*, add *more – more difficult*.

Go to page 128 for more information and practice.

Speaking

6 When you say sentences with *have to* you usually do not stress *to*.
Listen and repeat these sentences.

37
CD

1 I <u>have to</u> check my schedule.
2 She doesn't <u>have to</u> come.
3 He <u>has to</u> be on time.
4 I <u>have to</u> phone.
5 We don't <u>have to</u> do anything.
6 It <u>has to</u> work first time.

7 You telephone Colin, a colleague in Manchester. Read through the
prompts and responses before you press play. Play Track 38 and speak
after the beep. You start. Then listen to Track 39 to compare your
conversation.

38–39
CD

You	*(Say hello and ask about the weather.)*
Colin	Oh, hello! It's raining here!
You	*(Reply. Ask about his work.)*
Colin	Very busy!
You	*(Say you are visiting Manchester next week and ask if you can visit him.)*
Colin	Well, next week is busy, but I'm sure it's possible.
You	*(Ask what he's planning for Thursday.)*
Colin	Hmm, not so good. What are you doing on Wednesday?
You	*(Say you need to check your schedule.)*
Colin	No problem.
You	*(Ask when on Wednesday is good.)*
Colin	Wednesday morning is fine.

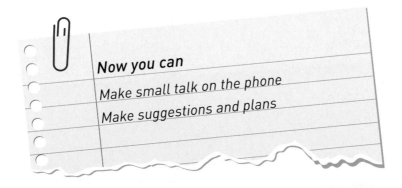

Now you can

Make small talk on the phone

Make suggestions and plans

13 Arranging the business trip

Writing a business email to arrange a visit | Asking your colleague to do something for you

Email

1   Read the email from Tom Field to John Carter and John's answer. How many nights does Tom plan to stay in Sydney?

Dear John

Following our phone call this morning, I have looked at my schedule and **the week starting** Monday October 20 is a good time for me to visit the APU offices in Sydney.

If you are happy with that, I'll arrive from London on the Friday before. **Would it be possible for** APU **to** book me a room in a hotel from October 17–24? I will fly back to London on October 25.

Regarding the agenda for our discussions, I could arrange a conference call with us three and also Diane to make a list of important topics. If you want, I'll invite other people as well, for example Robert Holden from the accounting department and Peter King from the legal department. **Please let me know.**

Best regards

Tom

Dear Tom

Thanks for your email. Yes, the dates are fine and we look forward to seeing you then. I think a telco in advance to agree your agenda with Diane is a good idea, but I don't think it's necessary to involve Robert and Peter at the moment. After the telco, Karen will set up some meetings with the relevant people here.

My assistant - Pia Levene - will organize your accommodation and she'll email you soon. By the way, would you like to do something on the Saturday evening? Maybe a harbour cruise and dinner? **Let me know if that's OK for you.**

Best wishes

John

Business tip

When you write an email to a colleague or partner in English, make sure you give yourself time to check it before you send it. Or even better, find someone else to check it for you.

Understanding

2   Read the emails again and answer these questions.

   1   What does Tom want APU to do?

   2   What two things does Tom suggest?

   3   What does John think about Tom's two suggestions?

   4   Who will reserve Tom a hotel room?

   5   What invitation does John make?

Key phrases

1 Emailing to make arrangements

Following our phone call … .	*Please let me know.*
Thanks for your email.	*Let me know if that's … .*
The week starting / ending … .	*Best regards / wishes, … .*
Regarding … . / As regards … .	

2 Asking for support / help

Would it be possible for … to … ?	

Practice

3 Complete the sentences with a word from the box.

> as   ending   for [x2]   if

1 Thanks very much _____ your email.

2 Let me know _____ that's OK.

3 _____ regards the meeting, here is the agenda.

4 Would it be possible _____ you to do it?

5 The week _____ March 5 is good for me.

4 Put the words in the sentences into the correct order.

1 OK / me / if / that / date / is / Let / know

_____.

2 ending / is / good / for / me / The / 25 / June / week

_____.

3 this / our / afternoon / here / are / my / Following / notes / meeting

_____.

4 your / for / phone / this / call / morning / Thanks

_____.

5 it / be / for / a / Would / room / you / to / possible / reserve / meeting

_____?

5 Read this email from John's assistant, Pia Levene. Find and correct the mistake in each numbered line.

Dear Mr Park

1 following your call yesterday with Mr Carter I have checked his schedule and

2 the week starting Febuary 14th is a good time for him to fly to Seoul.

3 Would it bee possible for you to collect Mr Carter from the airport to take him

4 to your offices? He will arrives on QA 673 from Sydney at 10.00 and will stay until February 20th.

5 As regard the agenda, Mr Carter asks if you will send him a list of the topics

6 you want to discuss. Please late me know if that is OK for you.

7 best regards

Pia Levene, Personal Assistant

Language spotlight

First conditional

If you are happy with that, I'll arrive … .
If you want, I'll invite … .
Conditional sentences have two parts: the condition clause and the result clause. We use the first conditional to talk about something that is likely to happen in the future:
If you send the report (condition), *I'll give it to my manager* (result).

Go to page 129 for more information and practice.

6   Yesterday you received an interesting email from a consultant, Kevin Murray. You write back to suggest a time when he can visit your office. Use these notes to help you.

   ● Thank him for his email.
   ● Say his services sound interesting.
   ● Ask if he can come to visit your office on 12th June in the morning to discuss working together.
   ● Say your assistant can reserve a hotel if he wants.
   ● Ask him to let you know if this is possible.

7   Now write a reply to this email. Use these notes to help you.
   Say 12th June is good for you.
   Reserving a hotel room is not necessary.
   Ask about the time of the meeting.

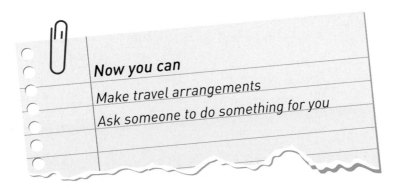

Now you can

Make travel arrangements
Ask someone to do something for you

14   Priorities for the business trip

Taking part in a telephone conference call | Prioritizing what to do

Telephone conference call

1   Tom, Diane, John and Karen take part in a telephone conference. Listen to the conversation. Who is the first person on the conference call?

40
CD

Recorded voice	A new participant is entering the call.
Tom	Tom Field here.
Karen	Hi, Tom. I'm here already. John is coming in a minute. How are you?
Tom	Oh, fine. How about you, Karen?
Karen	Great, thanks. I'm looking forward to ... .
Recorded voice	Two new participants are entering the call.
John	Hi Karen, hello Tom and Diane. John here.
Diane	And Diane as well. Hello everybody.
Tom	OK, we can start then. We need to make an agenda of topics for me to discuss next week with the guys from APU in Sydney.
Karen	Well, **first of all**, I want to show you the data centre. **That's very important.**
Tom	Yes. I agree. It's much bigger than the data centre in London, I think.
John	Right. And **next** you have to talk to Veronica Mayer. She's the data security manager.
Tom	OK.
Karen	**After that,** you must meet my team here. They can tell you about the developments we plan for our computer systems over the next five years. It's very exciting.

Tom	I'm sure. Then I can see what we have to do about our systems in London.
Karen	**Finally**, we have to decide when Lowis can change their accounting systems to the APU system. We can't wait too long. **That's crucial.**
Diane	Well, it looks like you're going to be busy, Tom!

Business tip

When you are visiting colleagues in another county, it is always a good idea to agree on an agenda of activities or itinerary before you travel there. This way you can make sure all the people you need to talk to are available for meetings.

Understanding

40
CD

2   Listen again and complete the agenda for Tom's visit to APU.

1   Visit to APU to see _____ .

2   Talk to Veronica Mayer the _____ manager.

3   Meet Karen's team to learn about new _____ for their computer systems.

4   Discuss timing of change to APU _____ systems.

Key phrases

Prioritizing

First of all ... / First .... / Firstly	*Third / Thirdly ... .*
Next	*Finally ... .*
Second / Secondly	*That's very important / crucial.*
After that, ...	

Practice

3   Join the two parts of the sentence together for these instructions on a coffee machine.

1	First of all,	**A**	put the money in the slot.
2	Second,	**B**	put your cup in the machine.
3	After that,	**C**	you can drink your perfect cup of coffee!
4	Finally,	**D**	choose the kind of coffee you want and press the button.

4 Complete the sentences.

1 After _____, you need to change your supplier.
2 Finally, we have _____ organize a workshop.
3 There are two problems: first, the product is too expensive and
  _____ the quality is bad.
4 These are my plans: first _____ all, I'm going to send the report
  and ...
5 That's very _____, crucial in fact.

5 A colleague of yours wants some tips about how to organize his day efficiently. Give him some ideas.

1 First of all, you need to _____ .
2 Next, you should _____ .
3 Third, you can _____ .
4 And finally you can _____ .

Language spotlight

Can for ability / possibility

We can start.
We can't wait.
We use can is used to talk about general ability or something that is possible in the present and future.

Go to page 130 for more information and practice.

Speaking

41
CD

6 Sometimes it is difficult to hear the difference between *can* and *can't*. Listen to these sentences and repeat them.

1 I can phone her.
2 I can't hear you.
3 They can't come today.
4 He can speak Japanese.
5 We can't pay them.
6 They can start work tomorrow.
7 When can you start?
8 Why can't you do it today?

7

**42–43
CD**

You are talking on the phone to a colleague, Jun Watanabe, who wants to come to visit your company. Read through the prompts and responses before you press play. Play Track 42 and speak after the beep. Then listen to Track 43 to compare your conversation.

Jun So I'm coming to visit you and other people next month. What topics should we discuss?

You *(1 / can / discuss / project schedule)*

Jun Good idea. What next?

You *(2 / have to check / project costs)*

Jun I agree. And after that?

You *(After / must talk about / problems with / consultants)*

Jun Yes, that is a big problem. Anything else?

You *(Finally / have to / go out for dinner)*

Jun That's a very good idea!

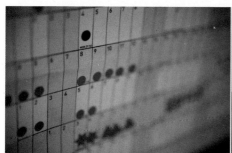 

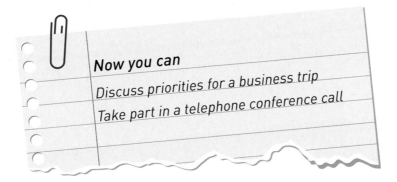

Now you can

Discuss priorities for a business trip

Take part in a telephone conference call

15 Dealing with questions in the conference call

Asking for repetition I Asking for explanations I Making recommendations

Telephone conference call

44
CD

1 Tom, Diane, John and Karen are still on a conference call. Listen to the conversation. What does Diane suggest and what does John think about her suggestion?

Diane	Well, we've agreed on Tom's agenda. But John, I think we should organize a conference for the senior management level of Lowis and APU. I think it could really help us all.
John	Hmm. **Is there a reason why** you think it's important at the moment?
Diane	Well, I think it would be a good idea for the managers to get together so that we can all see why changes at Lowis are so important.
John	**Yes, but I don't understand why** it's necessary for the managers from APU to take part as well. It'll be very expensive then.
Diane	Mmm, well it's clear that some things are not working as well as they could.
John	**I'm sorry but could you repeat that? I'm afraid I didn't hear what you said**.
Diane	Oh, sorry. I think if the people here meet the APU managers, everybody will be able to work together better.
Tom	And we can deal with some misunderstandings
Karen	**What do you mean by** 'misunderstandings'?
Tom	Well, we think we ought to improve the communication.
John	I see. **Can you give an example?**

Diane	Well, for some managers at Lewis it's difficult to understand why the changes are necessary. To the accounting systems, for example. We shouldn't wait until people here begin to cause problems.
John	Hmm. Yes, in that case maybe that is a good idea, Diane. I think you and I should send an invitation to the key people. When do you think would be a good date and where should we have the conference?

Business tip

Whenever you are unclear about what your business partner said in English, you should always ask them to explain it again. That way you can avoid misunderstandings. Be careful to sound polite when you ask these questions.

Understanding

44
CD

2 Listen again and choose the best answer.

1 Diane wants to organize a conference for
   A the old managers.
   B the managers with high positions in the company.
   C the young managers.

2 Diane wants to organize a conference so that
   A the APU managers understand what they have to do.
   B the Lewis managers understand what they have to do.
   C the APU and the Lewis managers understand what they have to do.

3 John wants
   A Karen to send the invitations.
   B Tom to send the invitations.
   C Diane and himself to send the invitations.

Key phrases

1 Asking for repetition

I'm sorry but could you repeat that?	I'm afraid / sorry I didn't hear what you said.

2 Asking for explanations

Is there a reason why ...?	What do you mean by ... ?
Yes, but I don't understand why	Can you give an example?

Practice

3 **Match the sentences.**

1 What do you mean by 'difficult'?
2 Can you give an example?
3 Could you repeat that?
4 Is there a reason why you're late?

A Sure. Last week I called your hotline and ...
B I said the 21st April.
C Well, my train was late.
D I mean it's not easy.

4 **Put the words in the sentences into the correct order.**

1 word / sorry / could / I'm / repeat / you / that / last / but

_____?

2 do / mean / you / by / 'delayed' / What

_____?

3 I / a / understand / But / why / it's / don't / problem

_____.

4 you / this / give / example / me / an / Can / of

_____?

5 **Complete the sentences.**

1 **A:** _____ understand. Why _____ difficult?
   B: It's difficult because we don't have the money.

2 **A:** Can _____ example?
   B: Yes, of course. The software doesn't work.

3 **A:** Is _____ you haven't paid us?
   B: Yes. We don't have any money at the moment.

4 **A:** _____ sorry. _____ that?
   B: Yes, I said 'delayed'.

5 **A:** _____ understand _____ her job is.
   B: Data security. She's the data security manager.

Language spotlight

Should / shouldn't / ought to for strong recommendations

We should organize a conference.
We ought to improve communication.
We shouldn't wait.
Should and *ought to* have the same meaning and are used to talk about things that are a good idea to do. *Shouldn't* is used when you want to say something is a bad idea.

Go to page 131 for more information and practice.

Speaking

6 When you ask for explanations, it is important to sound polite. Listen and repeat these sentences.

45
CD

1 Is there a reason why we can't do it this month?
2 Yes, but I don't understand why we have to wait.
3 What do you mean by a small delay?
4 Can you give an example?

7 You are talking on the phone to a supplier to your company about a problem. Read through the prompts and responses before you press play. Play Track 46 and speak after the beep. Then listen to Track 47 to compare your conversation.

46–47
CD

Supplier Then there was a strike at the factory.
You *(Ask him to repeat that.)*
Supplier There was a strike.
You *(Say you don't understand the word.)*
Supplier Oh, I see. A strike. It means the workers stopped working.
You *(Say you understand now. Ask why they had a strike now.)*
Supplier Well, they weren't happy with the new terms and conditions.
You *(Ask for an example.)*
Supplier Well, first the workers wanted more money.
You *(Ask for repetition. You didn't hear the last word.)*
Supplier The workers wanted more money.

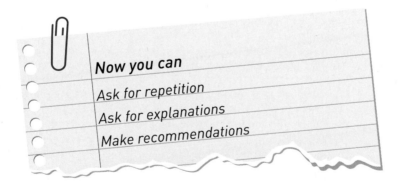

Now you can

Ask for repetition

Ask for explanations

Make recommendations

16   Written invitations

Writing a business invitation | Replying to a business invitation

Email

1   Diane and John agreed to organize a conference for the top managers of
APU and Lowis Engineering. Read the email invitation and reply. Where
and when will the conference take place? Can Ray Saunders attend?

Subject: **Save the date**

Dear **Colleagues**

We are pleased to invite you to the first joint senior management conference for
Australian Power Utilities and Lowis Engineering. **The event will take place on**
January 10 in London.

This occasion will be an opportunity to meet your new colleagues and network
with them. **We would be grateful if you could** email us if you can attend by
Wednesday November 4.

As soon as we receive your answer, we will send more information including a
detailed agenda, list of speakers, planned activities and hotel reservation forms.

We look forward to welcoming you to London **in the near future**.

Yours truly

Diane Kennedy & John Carter

Dear Diane and John

Thanks very much for your invitation to the conference. I think this is a very good idea.

I planned to go to our Brazil office during that week but will try to change this.

When I know I can change this trip, I will get back to you to confirm my attendance.

Best wishes
Ray Saunders

Business tip

When you write an important email to colleagues, make sure you get their attention with a phrase like *Save the date* as a subject heading.

Understanding

2   Read the email again. Are the sentences true (T) or false (F)?

1 The email is sent to customers of APU and Lowis.	T / F
2 Participants will have a chance to get to know each other.	T / F
3 Diane and John want people to telephone them with their answer.	T / F
4 The information about the conference is all on the email.	T / F
5 Participants will stay at a hotel.	T / F
6 Ray Saunders can definitely attend the conference.	T / F

Key phrases

A formal email invitation

Save the date	*We would be grateful if you … .*
Dear Colleagues	*We look forward to welcoming you to …*
We are pleased to invite you to … .	*in the near future*
The event will take place on … .	*Yours truly*
This occasion will be an opportunity to network with … .	

3 Find the word that is missing in each sentence.

    1 We are pleased invite you to the opening of our new offices in Penang.

    _____

    2 We would be grateful you inform us about you plans. _____

    3 We forward to welcoming you to our new offices in the near future. _____

    4 This occasion be an opportunity to meet senior managers. _____

4 Correct the mistake in each sentence.

    1 Please save the dade. _____

    2 The conference will take plaice on April 23. _____

    3 We look forward to seeing you in the next future. _____

    4 Yours Truly _____

    5 This conference will be an opportunity too meet the staff. _____

5 A colleague has written an invitation to customers for a sales conference to show your latest products. She wants you to check it. The highlighted parts are too informal. Rewrite the parts with more suitable, formal language.

> Dear Mr Hunter
>
> **1)** We want you to come to our sales conference on September 13. Please save the date.
>
> **2)** It's going to be in the Tower Hotel.
>
> **3)** It'll be a great chance for you to meet our staff.
> We look forward to welcoming you to London in the near future.
>
> **4)** Cheers,

1 _____

2 _____

3 _____

4 _____

Language spotlight

Time phrases

We use can phrases and words like *as soon as / when / after / before* to link sentences together.

As soon as we receive your answer, we will send an … .

When I know I can change this trip, I will get back to you to … .

Go to page 131 for more information and practice.

Writing

6 Your boss, James Scott, wants you to invite the senior management of your company to the opening of the company's new factory in Munich, Germany. Use his notes to write the invitation.

> Factory opening – April 4 (10:00 am)
> Opportunity to see new equipment in action
> Reply before March 1
> As soon as reply received – details of event, location and hotel
> Look forward to meet at factory opening

7 Write a reply to this invitation. Say you are not sure you can attend but will tell James as soon as you know.

Now you can

Write a business invitation

Reply to a business invitation

17 Business trip details

Providing hotel details | Talking about recent activities

Email

1 Pia Levene, John Carter's administrative assistant, sends an email to Tom. Why is she writing to him?

Dear Mr Field

Let me introduce myself – I am Mr Carter's administrative assistant and **I would like to confirm** your hotel arrangements.

I have booked you into the Southern Cross Hotel for seven nights (October 17-24). The hotel has sent me a confirmation code for your reservation, TF18OCT24210. The hotel has a limousine service and, if you send me your flight details, **I will arrange for** you to be picked up from the airport. **For detailed information about** the hotel facilities, **please check their website**:

www.southern-cross.aus

Mr Carter has reserved tickets for a performance of the opera *Carmen* at the Sydney Opera House on the Saturday evening. He will meet you in the hotel lobby at 6.30 pm. **You can find** reviews of the production here:

www.sydney_echo.com

I look forward to welcoming you to Sydney and the offices of APU on Monday October 20. **Please contact me if you have any questions.**

Yours sincerely

Pia Levene

Business tip

If you are organizing a business trip for an important foreign visitor, find out what their interests are – music, sport, theatre, museums, restaurants – so you can plan a social programme during their visit.

Understanding

2 Read the email again and answer these questions.

1 Who will pick Tom up from the airport?
2 What does Pia want Tom to send her?
3 Where can Tom find out if the hotel has a swimming pool?
4 Where will John take Tom on Saturday?

Key phrases

Looking after visitors

Let me introduce myself – I'm	*Please check ... .*
I would like to confirm	*You can find ... .*
I will arrange for	*Please contact me if you have any questions.*
For detailed information about	

Practice

3 Join the two parts of the sentences together.

1 I would like to confirm   **A** find information ... .
2 Please check your   **B** your reservation.
3 You can   **C** for your taxi to arrive at ... .
4 I will arrange   **D** information, please ... .
5 For detailed   **E** credit card details.

4   Put the words in the sentences into the correct order.

1   will / photocopied / documents / arrange / for / the / Jasmine / be / to

_____ .

2   I / to / Singapore Airport / like / would / your / landing / confirm / time / at.

_____ .

3   find / document / more / details / in / the / can / attached / You

_____ .

4   introduce / me / Let / myself / – / name's / Goodman / my / Jasmine

_____ .

5   call / any / you / me / if / have / Please / problems

_____ .

5   Read this email from Diane's assistant, Jasmine Goodman. Find and correct the mistake in each numbered line.

○ ○ ○

Dear Ms Taylor

(1) Let my introduce myself – I am Diane Kennedy's assistant and I am writing to you
(2) because I will like to confirm details about your visit next week.

(3) I have reserved meeting room 715 for you and I will arrange four coffee
(4) and water. A multimedia projector are available in the room for presentations.

(5) I have booked you into the Tower Hotel from October 12-15. For detail information,
(6) please cheque the hotel's website (**www.towerhotel.co.uk**).

(7) Please contact me if you has any questions.

Yours sincerely

Jasmine Goodman

(1) _____ (2) _____ (3) _____ (4) _____ (5) _____
(6) _____ (7) _____

Language spotlight

Present perfect

I **have booked** you into the Southern Cross Hotel for seven nights.
The hotel **has sent** me a confirmation code for your reservation.
Mr Carter **has reserved** tickets for a performance of the opera Carmen.
We use the present perfect to talk about recent activities.

Go to page 132 for more information and practice.

Writing

6 Your boss has asked you to email a new business contact, Kate Benders. Kate is going to visit your company to attend a meeting and go to dinner with your boss. Write to Ms Benders with these details.

- Introduce yourself.
- Hotel details: Harunami Hotel, three nights (March 23-26).
- Confirmation code: HH23MAR211
- Further information www.harunami_hotel.com
- Restaurant table reserved March 24. Boss will meet hotel lobby 7.00 pm
- Contact you with any questions.

Now you can

Give hotel details

Talk about recent activities

18   Changes to the schedule

Offering help | Making a request | Giving thanks

Telephone call

48
CD

1   Listen to Tom Field call Pia Levene in Sydney. How many days will Tom now stay in Australia?

Pia	Pia Levene, **how can I help you?**
Tom	Oh hello, Pia. This is Tom Field from Lowis Engineering in London.
Pia	Oh hello, Tom. **What can I do for you?**
Tom	Well, first of all, **thanks very much for** arranging my hotel for me.
Pia	My pleasure.
Tom	**I wonder if I could ask you for a favour**. **Could I make a small change** to the schedule?
Pia	Of course.
Tom	**Please could you change** my hotel reservation so that I arrive on October the 16th?
Pia	No problem.
Tom	And **I wanted to ask if you could arrange** for me to have a rental car for the Sunday, the 19th. I have some friends to visit up the coast. Just a small car.
Pia	Certainly. By the way, have you visited Sydney before, Tom?
Tom	No, I haven't.
Pia	Well, **would you like me to make sure** the rental company gives you a satnav in the car? So you don't get lost.
Tom	That's a great idea. **Thanks a lot for your help with all the arrangements,** Pia.
Pia	No worries.

| Tom | And **would you mind sending me an email** with the details again? **That would be really kind.** |
| Pia | Of course not. |

Understanding

48
CD

2 Listen to the conversation again. Pia wrote some notes during her conversation with Tom. What mistakes did she make?

1 Tom Field — Lowis Engineering
2 Wants to change hotel
3 Arrive Sydney Oct 16
4 Rental car 18-19 Oct
5 Visited Sydney already
6 Send letter confirming details

Key phrases

1 Offering help

| How can I help you? | Would you like me to ...? |
| What can I do for you? | |

2 Making a request

| I wonder if I can ask you for a favour? | I wanted to ask if you could ... . |
| Please could I / you change ...? | Would you mind sending me an email? |

3 Giving thanks

| Thanks very much for ...+ing | That would be really kind. |
| Thanks a lot for your help with the arrangements. | |

Practice

3 Match the sentences.

1 Would you like me to make reservations?
2 I wonder if I can ask you for a favour?
3 Thanks a lot for your help.
4 Please could you change the meeting room?
5 Would you mind saying that again?

A Of course. Which one would you like?
B My pleasure.
C Sure. What would you like me to do for you?
D For dinner? That would be really kind!
E Of course not.

4 Complete the sentences.

1 How _____ we help you?

2 I wanted to _____ if you could send me the files ...

3 _____ you like me to make sure they're sent by courier?

4 That would be really _____.

5 Thanks a _____ for your help with the project.

49
CD

5 Diane's assistant, Jasmine, is phoned by Eva Schmidt, about Eva's visit to Lowis Engineering next week. Put the sentences into the correct order to make a conversation. Then listen to Track 49 to check.

1	Jasmine	Jasmine Goodman, Lowis Engineering London. How can I help you?
	Eva	No, it's OK thank you. I'll take the underground. But thanks a lot for your help with the arrangements.
	Jasmine	Fine. Would you like me to organize for you to be met at the airport when you arrive?
	Eva	That's right.
	Jasmine	My pleasure!
	Eva	Well, you booked me a room at the Tower Hotel for three nights. Would you mind changing the reservation to only one night? For the last two nights I'm going to stay with friends.
	Jasmine	Of course, Ms Schmidt. What can I do for you?
	Eva	Hello. This is Eva Schmidt here. I wonder if I could ask you a favour.
	Jasmine	No problem. So you only want a room for October 31st?

Language spotlight

Present perfect - negatives and questions

Have you visited Sydney before?
Yes, I have. / No, I haven't.

We use the present perfect to ask and answer questions about past experiences where no specific time is mentioned.

Go to page 132 for more information and practice.

Speaking

6 When you ask people to do things for you and when you respond, it is important to sound polite. Listen and repeat these requests and responses.

50
CD

1 **A:** I wonder if I can ask you for a favour?
   B: Of course. How can I help?

2 **A:** Please could I change my reservation?
   B: No problem. I'll do that now.

3 **A:** I wanted to ask if you could send me a brochure.
   B: No worries. I'll do that today.

4 **A:** Would you mind sending me an email?
   B: Of course not.

7 You are calling Frank, an assistant to an important business partner, Mr Ho. You want to make changes to your planned visit to Mr Ho's company next week. Read through the prompts and responses before you press play. Play Track 51 and speak after the beep. Then listen to Track 52 to compare your conversation.

51–52
CD

Frank Frank Richards speaking.
You *(Say your name and ask if he can help you).*
Frank Of course. What can I do for you?
You *(Ask if you can change your meeting time with Mr Ho.)*
Frank I'm sure we can find a time. When is convenient?
You *(Ask if ten o'clock on Tuesday would be possible.)*
Frank Let me see ... well, I need to change another appointment of Mr Ho's, but that's not a problem.
You *(Great! Thank Frank for all his help with the arrangements.)*
Frank My pleasure!

Now you can

Change your plans

Ask for things

Thank people for their help

19 Welcome back to the office

Making small talk | Talking about a trip | Checking progress

Video

07
DVD

1 After Tom's trip to Australia, he meets his manager, Diane. Read the conversation and watch the video. What didn't Tom like about his flight?

Diane	Ah, Tom! **Good to see you again!**
Tom	Hello, Diane. **It's good to be back.**
Diane	**Good flight?**
Tom	Oh, **it was awful**! We had to land in a very cold Moscow because of a technical problem. We stayed there for six hours.
Diane	Oh, dear. **Well, it's nice to have you back. Is everything going well,** do you think, with APU? Did you get my email on Friday?
Tom	About the APU-Lowis joint management conference? Yes. I think the APU people are really interested in the idea. I can give you more details in the project meeting later.
Diane	Great. So, **what did you get up to** in Sydney? I remember they have some very good Italian restaurants.
Tom	Yeah! But the best restaurants were the Japanese sushi bars.
Diane	**Did you do any sightseeing?**
Tom	Yes, a little. John and his wife took me to Sydney Opera House to see *Carmen*.
Diane	**Lucky you!**
Tom	Yeah, it was a nice evening. My hotel room was overlooking Sydney harbour. It's the most amazing place.
Diane	**What was the weather like?**

| Tom | **Great**! Lots of sunshine and really hot. On the hottest day I think it was about thirty-five degrees. It rained here, didn't it? |
| Diane | Yes, every day last week! |

Business tip

When a colleague comes back to work from a business trip abroad or vacation, it's polite to make small talk about their trip. If you don't, they may feel you are not interested in them.

Understanding

07
DVD

2 Watch the video again and choose the best answer.

1 In Sydney, Tom
   A had a vacation.
   B worked all the time.
   C did some sightseeing.

2 Tom thinks the APU managers
   A like the idea of a joint conference.
   B don't like the idea of a joint conference.
   C are planning a joint conference.

3 Last week the weather was best in
   A Sydney.
   B London.
   C Moscow.

Key phrases

1 Making small talk

Good to see you again.	*Well, it's good / nice to have you back.*
It's good / nice to be back.	

2 Asking about and describing past experiences

Good flight?	*Lucky you!*
What did you get up to / do?	*It was awful!*
Did you do any sightseeing?	*Great!*
What was the weather like?	

3 Checking progress

Is everything going well with ... ?	*Is everything OK with ... ?*

3 Complete the sentences with language from Key phrases.

1 _____ to be back!   4 _____ you again!

2 _____ the weather like?   5 _____ get up to?

3 _____ any sightseeing?   6 _____ have you back!

4 Put the words in the sentences into the correct order.

1 did / get / Paris / up / you / to / What / in

_____?

2 the / like / weather / What / when / you / Seattle / were / was / in

_____?

3 she / there / do / any / Did / sightseeing / she / when / was

_____?

4 everything / in / going / Shanghai / Is / well

_____?

5 to / again / see / Good / you

_____!

5 Read the conversation between Robert and Jasmine. Put the sentences in the correct order. Then listen to Track 53 to check.

53
CD

	Robert	Some. I saw the Great Wall.
1	Robert	Hi Jasmine. Good to see you again!
	Robert	No, it was awful. But Bejing was great!
	Jasmine	Really? Did you do any sightseeing?
	Robert	Yes, Diane told me. But still, it's nice to be back!
	Jasmine	Fantastic! What was the weather like?
	Robert	Oh, great. On the hottest day it was about 35 degrees!
	Jasmine	Lucky you. It rained here.
	Jasmine	Hello, Robert. Nice to have you back! Good flight?

Language spotlight

Superlatives

But the best restaurants ... .   *It's the most amazing place.*
On the hottest day ... .

The superlative is formed like this: short words, for example *hot*, add *est* – *hottest*. Longer words, for example *amazing*, add *most* – *the most amazing*.

Go to page 128 for more information and practice.

Speaking

6 When you ask a question with *did you*, the two words are run together.
Listen and repeat the sentences.

54
CD

1 What <u>did you</u> say?
2 <u>Did you</u> go sightseeing?
3 <u>Did you</u> have a good flight?
4 When <u>did you</u> fly back?
5 How <u>did you</u> know?
6 What <u>did you</u> buy?

7 Your friend Cathy has just come back from a business trip to New York.
Talk to her. Read through the prompts and responses before you press
play. Play Track 55 and speak after the beep. Then listen to Track 56 to
compare your conversation.

55–56
CD

Cathy	Hello! Good to see you again.
You	*(Say it's nice to have her back again and ask if she had a good flight.)*
Cathy	Yes, it was fine.
You	*(Ask if everything is OK in the New York office.)*
Cathy	Yes. I had a very interesting time.
You	*(Ask if she went sightseeing.)*
Cathy	No, not really. But I did go shopping!
You	*(Lucky her! Ask her what she bought.)*
Cathy	Well, I went to Bloomingdale's because I've always wanted to go there. I bought a bag.
You	*(Ask about the weather there.)*
Cathy	Oh, it was good. Sunny and warm.
You	*(Say it was very cold here.)*
Cathy	Oh, dear.

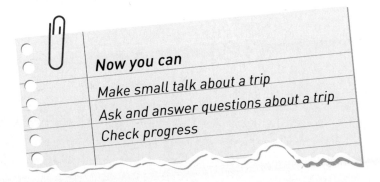

Now you can

Make small talk about a trip

Ask and answer questions about a trip

Check progress

20 The project review

Reviewing a project | Asking about work progress | Giving explanations

Video

1 Tom has to tell his manager, Diane, about the status of the IT integration project. Read the conversation and watch the video. Which task is behind schedule?

08
DVD

Diane	So, Tom, are you saying that John and Karen aren't happy about the project's progress?
Tom	Yes. They say we're too slow.
Diane	**Let's look at** the project plan then.
Tom	OK. So, **here we can see** all the main IT topics: integration of the human resources systems, the integration of accounting and bookkeeping and the integration of sales data.
Diane	**Can you show me** the project status?
Tom	**Well, the next diagram shows** the detailed schedule for all the HR systems: payroll, social security, performance review, training records. All integrated into the APU systems.
Diane	Great! Have you started the training programme for the HR people on the new system yet?
Tom	Oh, we've finished that already. We did that last month.
Diane	Good. So **when will you finish** everything else?
Tom	Well, **moving on to** the integration of our accounting systems, I'm afraid that's late. We haven't transferred all the data to APU yet.
Diane	Oh. **Can you explain why not?**
Tom	APU collects its information in a different way to us. That's one problem.

Diane	But **I don't understand why** that's a problem. It's the same information in different boxes.
Tom	The biggest problem is that Robert's accounting team is too small to do all the work. But I've told them they have to finish by the end of January.
Diane	Really? **When did you do that?**
Tom	I had a telephone conference call with them last week when I was in Sydney.
Diane	I see. That's good.
Tom	Moving on?
Diane	Sure.

Business tip

Don't be afraid of questions at a project review. It's a good sign because it shows interest in what you have to say. And it gives you a chance to deal with the points that interest people the most.

Understanding

08
DVD

2 Watch the video again. Are the sentences true (T) or false (F)?

1 John and Karen are happy with the project.   T / F
2 Tom has to bring the computer systems from Lowis and APU together. T / F
3 The training for the HR systems is finished.   T / F
4 The accounting systems are already integrated.   T / F
5 Robert doesn't have enough people.   T / F

Key phrases

1 Using slides in a project review	2 Asking questions at a project review
Let's look at … .	*Can you show me …?*
Here we can see … .	*Have you … yet?*
The next slide / diagram shows … .	*When will you finish …?*
Moving on to … .	*Can you explain why …?*
	I don't understand why … .
	When did you (do) that?

3 Join the two parts of the sentence together.

1	Have you finished	A	it's the most expensive company.
2	Let's look at	B	the second slide, we can see the problem.
3	I don't understand why	C	the figures.
4	Moving on to	D	the first part of the project?
5	When will you finish	E	the report yet?

4 A colleague at work is making a presentation about a project. Ask questions about the project and complete the sentences with your own information.

1 Can you show me _____?

2 I don't understand why _____?

3 When did you _____?

4 Have you written _____ yet?

5 When will you _____?

5 Tom has to make a presentation to his colleagues at Lowis about the project. Complete the sentence to go with each slide.

1	Schedule	_____ the project schedule.
2	Costs	_____ problems with the costs.
3	Quality	_____ question of quality, ...
4	Next steps	_____ next steps.

Language spotlight

Already and *yet*

Have you started the training programme yet?
Oh, we've finished that already.
I'm afraid we haven't transferred all the data to APU yet.
We use *yet* and *already* with the present perfect to ask and answer questions about recent activities.

Go to page 133 for more information and practice.

Speaking

6 An easy way to let your partner know what is the most important information in a sentence is by stressing a particular word. Stress can change the meaning of the sentence. Listen to these sentences.

57
CD

Have YOU finished the report? (YOU, nobody else)
Have you FINISHED the report? (Is the report completed?)
Have you finished the REPORT? (The REPORT, not the email)

Listen and repeat the sentences stressing the word in bold.

1 Have you **seen** Tom this afternoon yet? [meaning not spoken to him]
2 Have you seen **Tom** this afternoon yet? [meaning not Diane]
3 Have you seen Tom this **afternoon** yet? [meaning not this morning]
4 Have **you** seen Tom this afternoon yet? [meaning not someone else]

7 You are a manager and one of your team members is presenting information about her project. Ask her questions. Read through the prompts and responses before you press play. Play Track 58 and speak after the beep. Then listen to Track 59 to compare your conversation.

58–59
CD

Team member	So let's look at the project status then. Here we can see the costs so far.
You	*(Ask if she can show you the time schedule.)*
Team member	Yes, well the next slide shows the detailed schedule for the system integration and the training programme.
You	*(Ask if she has started the training programme yet.)*
Team member	No, we haven't started it yet.
You	*(Say you don't understand why not.)*
Team member	Well, the equipment isn't ready yet.
You	*(Ask when it will be ready.)*
Team member	It'll be ready by the end of this week. But we've finished the software update already.
You	*(Good! Ask when they did that.)*
Team member	That was on Friday last week.

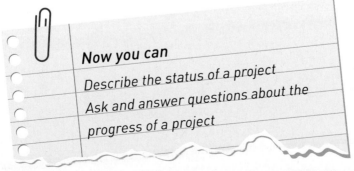

Now you can

Describe the status of a project

Ask and answer questions about the progress of a project

21 Starting the video conference

Taking part in a video conference | Describing technical problems | Dealing with delays

Video

09
DVD

1 **Tom and Diane in London start a video conference with John and Karen in Sydney. Read the conversation and watch the video. Can they solve the technical problem?**

Diane	So I just put in the numbers ... like that ... and then we should be able to see John and Karen. And there they are. This video conferencing equipment is fantastic! Hi John, hi Karen, can you hear us? **Sorry, your sound doesn't seem to be working!**
Karen	... and if we press this button, we should be able to hear them. Ah! There's Diane! Can you hear us?
Diane	That's much better.
Karen	**Just a moment.** Now **there seems to be something wrong with the picture.**
Karen	Diane, Tom? **I'm having trouble with the picture.** Can you see us?
Tom	Yes, and we can hear you too!
John	Well, **I think our system has crashed!** We can't see anything!
Karen	Oh, I don't understand. **When I click on the start button, nothing happens.**
John	**Sorry to keep you waiting, Diane.** Karen can't work this thing and I don't know what to do either.
Karen	**I think I need to call a technician. Hold on a minute!**
Diane	Don't worry. I completely understand. We can wait.

Business tip

If you need to use technical equipment for presentations, conferences or meetings then make sure:

1 that you have checked the equipment is working at least half an hour before you need it.

2 you have the telephone number of somebody who can help you if things go wrong.

Understanding

09
DVD

2 Watch the DVD again and answer the questions.

1 Who has a problem with their technical equipment, Diane and Tom or Karen and John?

2 What is their problem?

3 What do they do about their problem?

Key phrases

1 Describing technical problems	2 Dealing with delays
There seems to be something wrong with … .	*Just a moment.*
I'm having trouble with … .	*Hold on a minute.*
I think my XYZ has crashed.	*Sorry to keep you waiting.*
The XYZ doesn't seem to be working.	
When I click on the XYZ, nothing happens.	
I think I need to call a technician.	

Practice

3 Complete the sentences with information from the box.

| click | keep | on | trouble | wrong |

1 Sorry to _____ you waiting.

2 When I _____ on the Word icon, nothing happens!

3 There seems to be something _____ with the remote control.

4 Hold _____ a minute, please.

5 I'm having _____ with my cell phone.

4 Put the words in the sentences into the correct order.

1 We're / server / having / with / trouble / the

_____ .

2 need / think / to / I / call / the / we / help / desk

_____ .

3 a / Just / please / moment,

_____ .

4 I / email / my / open / account, / When / computer / crashes / my

_____ .

5 telephone / to / seem / The / doesn't / working / be

_____ .

5 What do you say to the computer service hotline when:

1 Your computer has a blue screen?
   My system _____ .
2 The computer is working but you can't open your email account?
   I'm having _____ .
3 You can't print a document?
   There seems _____ .
4 Your internet connection isn't working?
   The internet doesn't _____ .
5 You have to check your computer details before you can answer a question?
   Sorry _____ .

Language spotlight

Too* and *not ... either

Yes, and we can hear you <u>too</u>!
Karen <u>can't</u> work this thing and I <u>don't</u> know what to do <u>either</u>.
Too has the same meaning as *as well* or *also*. It is usually placed at the end of the sentence. If we want to use the negative form, we use *not ... either*.

Go to page 133 for more information and practice.

Speaking

6 When somebody tells you something bad has happened to them, you
need to be able to react to it. Listen and repeat these phrases.

60
CD

1 Oh no!

2 Sorry to hear that!

3 That's terrible!

4 I am sorry!

5 That's awful!

7 You have a problem with your computer and you call a service hotline
to ask for help. Read through the prompts and responses before you
press play. Play Track 61 and speak after the beep. Then listen to
Track 62 to compare your conversation.

61–62
CD

Help desk	How can I help you?
You	*(Tell her there is something wrong with your computer.)*
Help desk	OK. What's the matter?
You	*(Say you're having trouble with the screen.)*
Help desk	OK. Have you tried to reboot your computer?
You	*(Say when you click on the restart icon nothing happens.)*
Help desk	Have you tried to turn off the computer and then restart?
You	*(Ask her to wait a moment.)*
Help desk	No problem.
You	*(Say you are sorry to keep her waiting. Then say you need a technician.)*
Help desk	OK, I'll come up to your office.
You	*(Say thanks.)*

Now you can

Start a video conference

Deal with technical problems

22 Discussing problems in the video conference

Agreeing in meetings I Disagreeing in meetings

Video

10
DVD

1 After the technical difficulties are sorted out, Tom, Diane, John and Karen continue their video conference to discuss problems with the integration of Lowis into APU. Read the conversation and watch the video. What doesn't Diane want to do?

John	Oh good! We can see and hear you now! Thanks, Tony.
Diane	Excellent! So we need to discuss the progress of the project, I think.
Karen	**That's right.** The integration of the human resources and the sales departments has gone well. It's just your accountants that are a problem. They don't seem to want to use our IT accounting system so they do everything slowly!
Diane	**I don't agree**, Karen. Our accountants have to check your system carefully to be sure ...
Karen	**Yes, but** it's three months now! I think you need to put more pressure on Robert Holden's team.
Tom	**I'm not sure that's going to work.** They don't have enough people for all their tasks at the moment. They need help.
Diane	**I think so too.** They need more resources, not more pressure.
John	Maybe I should talk to Robert and explain why it's so important.
Diane	Look, **I'm sorry but I don't think that's a good idea**. Robert knows why it's important. We just have to give him more time.
Karen	**I'm afraid that's not possible.** We have to integrate the systems before the new financial year starts in January.
John	**Yes, I agree**. You can't run a business without financial information.
Diane	**You're absolutely right.** So let's see if we can find another solution to this problem.

Business tip

Agreeing and disagreeing in business life is normal. But the way people agree and disagree with each other is different from culture to culture. If you are in meetings with partners from a different culture to yours, make sure you understand in advance how people in that culture show agreement or disagreement.

Understanding

10
DVD

2 Watch the video again. Are the sentences true (T) or false (F)?

1 The accounting department integration is going well.   T / F
2 Karen thinks the accounting department is working slowly.   T / F
3 Diane agrees with Karen.   T / F
4 The accounting team has enough people.   T / F
5 Diane wants to find a solution to the problem.   T / F

Key phrases

1 Agreeing	2 Disagreeing
That's right.	*I don't agree.*
Yes, I agree.	*Yes, but ... .*
I think so too.	*I'm not sure that's going to work.*
You're absolutely right.	*I'm sorry but I don't think that's a good idea.*
	I'm afraid that's not possible.

Practice

3 Join the two parts of the sentence together.

1 She's absolutely   A   too.
2 We're not sure   B   right.
3 I'm afraid   C   agree.
4 They think so   D   that's going to work.
5 He doesn't   E   that's not possible.

4 Complete the sentences.

1 Mr Brauer isn't _____ that's going to work.
2 I'm _____ but we don't think that's a good idea.
3 I'm afraid that's _____ possible.
4 They're _____ right.
5 We think _____ too.

5 Tom is in a meeting with two colleagues, Simon and Fiona. Put the sentences into the correct order to make a conversation. Then listen to Track 63 to check.

63
CD

_1_	Fiona	We need to open a new office in Moscow for our Russian customers. What do you think?
	Simon	Yes, I agree. We need to be close to our customers.
	Fiona	I'm sorry but I don't think that's a good idea, Simon!
	Tom	Yes, but at the moment we don't have any customers there, do we?
	Simon	We need to remember the costs. You're quite right. Perhaps we should close the office in Sydney and then open an office in Moscow.
	Simon	I don't agree. We have some business with Vladivoil. We need to increase that.
	Tom	I'm sorry but I don't think it's a good idea. It's very expensive to open an office in Russia.
	Fiona	I think so too. Russia is the next big market.

Language spotlight

Adverbs

They do everything so <u>slowly</u>!
Our accountants have to check your system <u>carefully</u>.
The integration ... has gone <u>well</u>.
An adverb describes a verb. We form regular adverbs by adding *–ly* to an adjective, for example *strongly – strongly*, or *–ily* to adjectives ending in *y*, for example *pretty - prettily*. The adjective *good* is an exception and has the adverb *well*.

Go to page 134 for more information and practice.

Speaking

6 When you disagree with someone, it is important to sound polite. Listen and repeat these sentences.

64
CD

1 I'm sorry but I don't agree with you.

2 Yes, but that's too late, I'm afraid.

3 I'm not sure that's going to work.

4 I'm sorry but I think that's a bad idea.

5 I'm afraid that just isn't going to be possible.

7
65–66
CD

You are having a meeting with Dale, a colleague from the US, to discuss IT strategy for your company. Read through the prompts and responses before you press play. Play Track 65 and speak after the beep. Then listen to Track 66 to compare your conversation.

Dale Well, the next point on the agenda is IT strategy. We need to decide what to do next about our business management system.

You *(Agree.)*

Dale In the US we think we need to update our business management system.

You *(Disagree and say you think the present system is fine.)*

Dale But the new system is really easy to use!

You *(Disagree and say you think the new system has problems.)*

Dale Well, the present system does work well.

You *(Agree.)*

Dale But the new system is much faster.

(Suggest you continue the discussion at lunch.)

Dale Good idea!

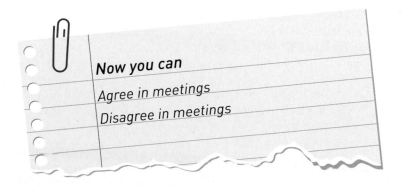

Now you can

Agree in meetings

Disagree in meetings

23 Finding solutions in the video conference

Summarizing the situation | Making proposals | Discussing possibilities

Video

11
DVD

1 Tom, Diane, John and Karen continue their video conference to discuss problems with the integration of Lowis into APU. Read the conversation and watch the video. What does Diane suggest?

Diane	**So, this is the situation:** you want the Accounting department here at Lowis to integrate our IT systems into APU's. But we don't have enough people to do it quickly and, if it isn't finished before the new financial year, we'll have a problem. So, **what can we do?**
Karen	**What about** hiring extra IT people?
John	I don't think that's going to work.
Tom	I agree with you, John. IT people can be expensive and, anyway, they don't know our two companies.
Diane	That's what I think. It'll take too long to explain everything. But **what if you** send over some of your accountants to help Robert's team?
Tom	Good idea. And **how about** sending some IT specialists too?
John	Well, **we could always** see if there are some IT people here who are able to do it if that's really necessary.
Karen	But first, **why don't you** check with Robert what extra help he needs with the new system?
John	Good point, Karen. Tom, can you send over some information as to where the problem is exactly?
Tom	I'll do that today.
Diane	Excellent. And John, if we tell you who we need, will you send us your people quickly?
John	We'll do our best. This is important.

Business tip

When you are looking for new ideas to solve a problem, one good technique is *brainstorming*. In brainstorming meetings people first share their ideas and write them on a flipchart or whiteboard. After everyone has given their ideas, the people in the meeting then discuss the ideas.

Understanding

11
DVD

2 Watch the video again and choose the best answer.

1 The Accounting department at Lowis Engineering
   A has too many people.
   B hires consultants.
   C needs more people to do the integration work.

2 Tom and Diane think that extra IT people
   A are expensive and need too much time to do the work.
   B will do the job well.
   C could be a good idea.

3 Karen wants to know
   A who Robert is.
   B what help Robert needs with the new systems.
   C when Tom can contact her.

4 John wants Lowis to send to APU
   A some information about the people and the problem.
   B some information about the people.
   C some information about the problem.

Key phrases

1 Summarizing the situation

So, this is the situation:	*So, to sum up:*

2 Making proposals

What about -ing ... ?	*How about -ing ... ?*
What if you ...?	*Why don't you ... ?*

3 Discussing possibilities

What can we do?	*We could always ... .*
We can (do this) or we can (do that).	

---

3 Join the two parts of the sentence together.

1	We can send it by mail	A always stay in a hotel.
2	He could	B say to her?
3	Why doesn't	C or we can courier the package.
4	What can I	D finishing the report first?
5	What about	E she telephone him?

4 Put the words in the sentences into the correct order.

1 about / new / trainer / hiring / How /a _____?

2 could / ask / it's / important / always / him / We / if _____.

3 don't / meeting / you / arrange / Why / another _____?

4 can / situation / we / about / do / What / the _____?

5 changing / about / systems / our / What / computer _____?

5 Put the conversation between Tom and his colleague Robert Holden into the correct order. Then check your answer with the Track 67.

1	Tom	So, Robert, what can we do about the IT integration problem?
	Tom	No, APU says it must be this year. What else can we do?
	Robert	Of course. If this doesn't work, I'll lose my job!
	Tom	That's too expensive. How about asking people at APU to help?
	Robert	Good idea!
	Robert	We could always hire some extra people.
	Tom	Can you give me a list of the people you need?
	Robert	What if we ask APU if we can do the integration next year?

(67 CD)

Language spotlight

First conditional negative and question forms

If it isn't finished before the new financial year, we'll have a problem.
If it's finished before the new financial year, we won't have a problem.
If we tell you who we need, will you send us your people quickly?

To make a negative, we either add *not* / *don't* / *doesn't* to the *if* clause or *not* to the result clause. To ask questions we turn the result clause into the question form.

Go to page 129 for more information and practice.

Speaking

6 Listen to these questions and repeat them. Note the key words to stress.

68
CD

1 What can we **do**?
2 What about **hiring** extra **people**?
3 What if you send some of your **accountants** to help Robert's **team**?
4 How about some IT specialists **too**?
5 Why don't you check with **Robert** what help he needs?
6 Can you send me some **information** about the problem?

69–70
CD

7 You and a colleague, Angie, have to organize the new English training programme for your company. Discuss together the different possibilities. Read through the prompts and responses before you press play. Play Track 69 and speak after the beep. Then listen to Track 70 to compare your conversation.

Angie	Well, we need to decide what to do about the English training. What do you think we can do?
You	*(Suggest sending people to the UK or Australia.)*
Angie	I think that's too expensive.
You	*(Suggest hiring an English teacher.)*
Angie	But it's difficult to know if they are good English teachers.
You	*(Suggest working with a good school.)*
Angie	Yes, that's a good idea. What should I do next?
You	*(Suggest she checks how many people want to study English.)*
Angie	Good idea!

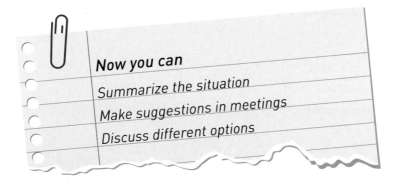

Now you can

Summarize the situation

Make suggestions in meetings

Discuss different options

24   Ending the video conference

Ending a meeting | Arranging a new appointment | Saying goodbye

Video

12
DVD

1 Tom, Diane, John and Karen have nearly finished their video conference. Read the conversation and watch the video. When is their next video conference?

John	So, **have we covered everything** today?
Diane	**Yes. I think that covers everything.**
John	**So to recap**, I'm going to tell the head of the Accounting department here that some of his experts must be flown to London for a few weeks.
Karen	And I'll check which of our IT specialists can be sent to you as well.
Diane	Fantastic! With this solution I really think the accounting systems will be integrated on time.
John	Great! Would it be possible to have someone arrange the hotels and security passes for our team?
Diane	No problem. My PA, Jasmine, will handle that.
John	Ah yes, Jasmine! So, **when should we next meet?**
Tom	**When is a good time for you?**
John	OK, **let me check my schedule.** Ah, how is this time Thursday next week for you?
Diane	**That's good for me.**
Tom	Me, too.

Karen	And me!
Tom	Should I send invitations and set up the video conference?
John	Ah, yes, thanks Tom, that would be great. So, we'll be in touch soon. And next week, Diane, we must discuss the senior management conference.
Diane	Excellent idea. I look forward to it. Bye then!
Tom	**See you next week then.**
Karen	Bye
John	Take care!

Business tip

Before you finish a meeting, it is a good idea to recap on the main points to make sure that everyone understands what has been agreed. It is also important to make sure everyone is clear about their own action points.

Understanding

12
DVD

2 Watch the video again and correct some of the action points that Tom made for himself during the video conference.

- John will ask for accounting specialists to fly to London.
- Diane will look for IT specialists.
- Jasmine will arrange hotels and security passes for team.
- I will set up video conference for Tuesday next week.

Key phrases

1 Ending a meeting

Have we covered everything today?	*I think that covers everything.*
So to recap, … .	

2 Arranging a new appointment

When should we next meet?	*When is a good time for you?*
Let me check my schedule.	*Does XYZ suit you?*
That's good for me!	*See you next week then.*

3 Complete the sentences with words from the box.

covered	her	include	See	suit	think	When

1 When is a good time for _____?
2 Does Friday two pm _____ you?
3 I _____ that covers everything.
4 _____ should we next meet?
5 Have we _____ everything?
6 _____ you tomorrow.

4 Put the words in the sentences into the correct order.

1 Monday / you / next / afternoon / Does / week / suit _____?
2 me / my / schedule / Let / check / month / for / next _____.
3 good / time's / for / That / us _____.
4 to / our / recap / discussions / So / today _____, ...
5 is / time / a / for / Mr / When / good / Holden _____?

5 Write a phrase or sentence which would be most useful in the following situations.

1 You want to check the points agreed in the meeting.

_____

2 You think that all the points have been discussed.

_____

3 You want to arrange another meeting.

_____

4 You want to check your schedule.

_____

5 You want to suggest a time.

_____

6 Say that a time is suitable for you.

_____

Language spotlight

Passive

Some experts <u>must be flown</u> to London.
I'll check which of our IT specialists <u>can be sent</u>.
I think the accounting systems <u>will be integrated</u> on time.
We use the passive when the action is more interesting or more important than the person who has to perform the action.

Go to page 135 for more information and practice.

Speaking

6 When you want to show you like an idea, it is important to sound enthusiastic. Listen and repeat these words or phrases.

71
CD

1 That's good!
2 Fantastic!
3 Great!
4 Excellent idea!

7 You and a colleague have almost finished a meeting. Read through the prompts and responses before you press play. Play Track 72 and speak after the beep, using the prompts to help you. Then listen to Track 73 to compare your conversation.

72–73
CD

Tony	Well, have we covered everything?
You	*(Yes / think / cover / everything.)*
Tony	So, to recap. My team must be trained to use the new system. And the trainers can be provided by this company, xSoft. Is that correct?
You	*(Yes. When / next / meet?)*
Tony	Let me check my schedule.
You	*(Tuesday / four o'clock?)*
Tony	Sorry, no. How about two o'clock?
You	*(Good)*
Tony	Great. Shall we go for a coffee? I need one!
You	*(Agree)*

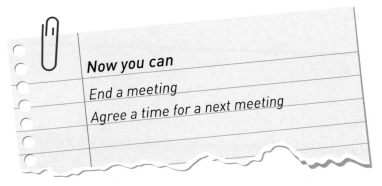

Now you can

End a meeting

Agree a time for a next meeting

Greeting colleagues

Good morning / Morning! / Good afternoon. / Afternoon!
Hi!
Hello, …. How are you?
Fine thanks, and you?
Very well!

Talking about your weekend

Good weekend?
Great, thanks!
How was your weekend?
Very busy!

Making small talk

Good to see you again.
It's good / nice to be back.
Well, it's good / nice to have you back.

Asking about and describing past experiences

Good flight? / How was the flight?
What did you get up to / do?
Did you do any sightseeing?
What was the weather like?
Lucky you!
It was awful!
Great!

Welcoming company guests and exchanging business cards

Good to see you again!
Good to see you again too.
Can I introduce you to …?
Nice to meet you.
Nice to meet you too.
Please, call me XYZ.
Let me introduce ….
Pleased to meet you both.
Pleased to meet you too.
Let me give you my card.
Here's my card.
What do you do?

Offering refreshments to guests

Help yourself to something.
Could you pass me ...?
Sorry, is that chicken?
I'm afraid I don't eat meat.
Would you like some ...?
Have some ... .
It's delicious.

Starting meetings and making requests

Thank you for coming to this meeting.
Let's start by *+ing* ... .
I want you to ... .
I would / I'd like you to ... .
We really need you to ... .
Could you ...?
Would you mind if I ...?

Checking progress

Is everything going well with ...?
Is everything OK with ...?

Using slides in a meeting / presentation

Let's look at ... .
Here we can see ... .
The next slide shows ... .
Moving on to ... .

Asking questions in a meeting

Can you show me ...?
Have you ... yet?
When will you finish ...?
Can you explain why ...?
I don't understand why ... .
When did you (do) that?
Can you tell me ...?
Why do you have ...?
How much ...?
How many ...?

Agreeing

That's right.
Yes, I agree.
I think so too.
You're absolutely right.

Disagreeing

I don't agree.
Yes, but … .
I'm not sure that's going to work.
I'm sorry but I don't think that's a good idea.
I'm afraid that's not possible.

Summarizing the situation

So, this is the situation: … .
So, to sum up: … .

Making proposals

What about -ing …?
How about -ing …?
What if you / we …?
Why don't you/we …?

Discussing possibilities

What can we do?
We could always … .
We can do this or we can do that.

Ending a meeting

Have we covered everything today?
I think that covers everything.
Are you OK with that?
So to recap, … .
Let me summarize: … .
I think that's enough for today.

Arranging a new appointment

When should we next meet?
When is a good time for you?
Let me check my schedule.
Does XYZ suit you?
That's good for me!
See you next week then.

Starting a presentation

I would like / I'd like to tell you something about … .
First, … . / First of all, … .
Second, … .
Third, … .
Next … .
Finally, … .

Questions and answers at a presentation

Do you have any questions?
Sorry, I don't understand your question.
I'm glad you asked that question.
That's a good question.
I'm not sure about that.
(Now) I have a question for you, Tom.
Let me think.

Talking about the past

After ..., we did ... .
Then ... .

Calling a business partner

Hello, this is Tom Field from ... .
Can I speak to Karen Taylor, please?
Can you put me through to ...?
I'll call back later.
I'll send her an email.
Thanks for your help.

Answering the phone

Kim Benders speaking. / This is Kim Benders speaking. / Kim Benders.
I'm afraid she's not in the office.
She's on a business trip to ... .
Can I help you?
Hold the line, please. / Can you (please) hold?
I'm sorry but his line's busy at the moment.
Can I take a message?

Starting telephone conferences

Tom here.
I'm sitting here with Karen.
I'm calling from home.
I'm working at / from home today.
Diane will call in in a minute.
Sorry we're late.
Let's start.

Key phrases for speaking

Describing technical problems in telephone and video conferences

There seems to be something wrong with ….
I'm having trouble with ….
I think my XYZ has crashed.
The XYZ doesn't seem to be working.
When I click on the XYZ, nothing happens.
I think I need to call a technician.

Dealing with delays

Just a moment.
Hold on a minute.
Sorry to keep you waiting.

Telephone small talk

How's the weather …?
How's work at the moment? / What's work like at the moment?
Did you see the football / basketball game last night?
What are you doing this weekend?
What are your plans for this weekend?
It's raining here.
Sounds great.
Too bad.

Making suggestions and arrangements

I was wondering if you could ….
When is a good time for you?
I have to check my schedule.

Making arrangements

I just want to let you know ….
What are your plans on …?
Let me check my schedule for next week.
How does Monday afternoon look?
Let me take a look.

Prioritizing

First of all …. / First …. / Firstly ….
Next….
Second / Secondly ….
After that, ….
Third / Thirdly ….
Finally ….
That's very important / crucial.

Asking for repetition

I'm sorry but could you repeat that?
I'm afraid / sorry I didn't hear what you said.

Asking for explanations

Is there a reason why ...?
Yes, but I don't understand why ... .
What do you mean by ...?
Can you give an example?

Offering help

How can I help you?
What can I do for you?
Would you like me to ...?

Making a request

I wonder if I can ask you for a favour?
Could you do me a favour?
Please could I / you change ...?
I wanted to ask if you could ... .
Would you mind sending me an email?

Giving thanks

Thanks very much for ... +ing ... .
Thanks a lot for your help with the arrangements.
That would be really kind.

Saying goodbye

Good to speak to you, ...
Speak to you soon.
Nice speaking to you, ...
I'm looking forward to it.

Key phrases for writing

Business emails

I tried to call / phone you ... but ... .
With regard to ... ,
I look forward to speaking to you soon.

Best wishes

Making suggestions and appointments

I think it's a good idea if ... .
I suggest that I ... .
Could you let me know if that's convenient for you?

Emailing to make arrangements

Following our phone call, ...
Thanks for your email.
The week starting / ending ... .

Regarding ... . / As regards ... .

Please let me know.
Let me know if that's ... .

Best regards / wishes, ...

Automated replied

I am out of the office [in ...] until ... .

Making suggestions

Why don't I ...?
If this is OK for you, ...
Perhaps we could ... .

Requests and asking for opinions

How do you feel about this? / What's your opinion about ...?
Shall we ...?
Do you think you could ...? / Would you mind +*ing* ...?

Asking for support / help

Would it be possible for ... to ...?

Looking after visitors

Let me introduce myself – I'm ... .

I would like to confirm ... .
I will arrange for... .
For detailed information about ... .
Please check ... .
You can find ... .
Please contact me if you have any questions.

Formal email invitations

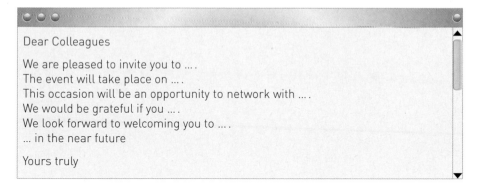

Dear Colleagues

We are pleased to invite you to ... .
The event will take place on ... .
This occasion will be an opportunity to network with ... .
We would be grateful if you ... .
We look forward to welcoming you to ... .
... in the near future

Yours truly

Key words

Companies

	Your translation
boss	
branch	
colleague / co-worker	
department	
division	
employee	
employer	
headquarters	
job	
to manage	

Departments

	Your translation
Accounting	
Customer Services	
Distribution	
Human Resources [HR]	
Information Technology (IT)	
Logistics	
Marketing	
Payroll	
Production	
Research and Development	
Sales	
Security	
Transport [UK] / Transportation [US]	
Warehousing	

Events and meetings	
	Your translation
agenda	
agreement	
boardroom	
catering	
change	
compromise	
conference room	
equipment	
event	
facilities	
flip chart	
invitation	
meeting room	
negotiation	
participant	
presentation	
projector	
time out	
to agree	
to argue	
to arrange	
to attend	
to book	
to bring forward	
to cancel	
to disagree	
to make a deal	
to invite	
to negotiate	
to organize	
to put / move back	
to reserve	

Key words

In the office

	Your translation
chair	
computer	
cubicle / work station	
desk	
fax machine	
hole punch (UK) / hole puncher (US)	
paper	
paper clip	
pen	
pencil	
photocopy / copy	
printout	
stapler	
stationery	
telephone / phone	
to email	
to fax	
to forward	
to print something [out]	
to staple	

Emails

	Your translation
disclaimer	
greeting	
out-of-office notice	
recipient	
sender	
subject	
to CC	
to contact	
to delete	
to email	
to forward	

Office job titles

	Your translation
administrative assistant	
chairman / chairwoman / chair / chair person	
chief executive officer [CEO]	
chief financial officer [CFO]	
Chief operating officer [COO]	
clerk	
consultant	
engineer	
lawyer	
manager	
managing director	
personal assistant	
receptionist	
salesman / saleswoman / salesperson / sales rep [representative]	
secretary	

Telephoning

	Your translation
busy (line)	
cell (US) / mobile (UK) phone	
engaged (line) (UK)	
extension	
line	
mobile (UK) phone / cell phone (US)	
to call (US)	
to call back	
to connect someone to someone	
to hold (the line)	
to put someone through to someone	

Key words

Travel	
	Your translation
flight	
car hire (UK) / car rental (US)	
journey	
plane	
subway (US) / underground (UK)	
taxi	
tour	
traffic	
train	
trip	

Presentations	
	Your translation
audience	
conclusion	
handout	
laser pointer	
multimedia projector	
overview	
slide	
screen	
to make a presentation	
to present	
to sum up	

Projects	
	Your translation
Act of God	
budget	
clause	
client	
contract	
cost	
customer	
deadline	
delay	
delivery	
goal	
kick-off meeting	
main contractor	
penalty	
phase	
plan	
progress	
project	
project leader / manager / member / team	
project meeting	
project room	
quality	
resources	
schedule	
status	
strike	
subcontractor	
supplier	
time	
timeline	

Present continuous

Positive forms:

- I'm [I am] **waiting** for my taxi.
- We're [We **are**] **staying** at the Anchor Hotel.
- They're [They **are**] **having** a meeting.

Negative forms:

- No, I'm not **staying** in the country.
- She **isn't** [She is not] waiting for Diane.

Questions:

- **Are** you **staying** at the Anchor Hotel?
- **Is** Mr Jones **waiting** to see me?
- When are they **leaving**?

Long answers:

- Yes. I'm **staying** at the Anchor.
- No, I'm not **staying** in London.

Short answers:

- Yes, I **am**.
- Yes, she **is**.
- Yes, they **are**.
- No, I'm **not**.
- No, she **isn't**.
- No, they **aren't**.

This tense is used to describe an action that is happening NOW:

- Would you like an umbrella because it's **raining** (now)?

Or an action that has started but is not finished:

- I'm **waiting** to see him.

It is also used for temporary actions or situations:

- She's **staying** at the Anchor Hotel in London for three nights.

Words that often take the present continuous are: *now, at the moment, presently.*

Future meaning

The present continuous can have a future meaning and is used to talk about future activities that have been arranged or planned.

- I'm **staying** in the hotel next week too.
- We're **playing** golf with Yoshi on Saturday.
- He's **meeting** them on Monday.
- He's not **flying** to New York until after Friday the 13th.
- **Are** you **giving** a talk at the data security conference next month?
- **Is** he **coming** to Germany soon?

If we use this form, we know the plans are fixed so it's a good way to make an excuse.

- Sorry, I can't come on Monday. I'm **driving** to Frankfurt.

Watch out – we don't usually use these verbs in the continuous form: *remember, understand, want, like, belong, suppose, need, seem, prefer, believe, know, think (= believe), hear, smell, have (= possess).*

Exercise 1

Complete the text with the present simple or present continuous forms of the verbs in parentheses.

Tom Field and Diane Kennedy both 1) _____ (work) for Lowis Engineering. At the moment Diane 2) _____ (focus) on the integration of Lowis Engineering into APU and Tom 3) _____(help) her. Tom usually 4) _____ (arrive) at work at about 8.30 am, but today he 5) _____ (stay) at home because he 6) _____(not feel) well.

Exercise 2

Put the words in the sentences into the correct order.

1 APU / is / next / visiting / the / Diane / offices / month.
2 going / Aren't / to / the / you / Saturday / party / on?
3 afraid / we're / I'm / visiting / mother / this / my / weekend.
4 isn't / Tuesday / arriving / She / until.
5 o'clock / meeting / at / They're / the / President / three.
6 he / flying / Is / soon / to / LA?

Present simple

Positive forms:

- I **work** at the reception desk.
- She **enjoys** her job very much.
- Our employees **love** helping visitors.

Negative forms:

- I **don't [do not] work** for Lowis Engineering.
- This visitor **doesn't [does not]** have a security card.
- We **don't allow** pets in the company.

Questions:

- **Does** she **work** for Lowis Engineering?
- Where **do** you **come** from?

Long answers:

- Yes, she **does work** for Lowis Engineering.
- No, she **doesn't work** for Lowis Engineering.

Short answers:

- Yes, I **do**.
- No, I **don't**.
- Yes, she **does**.
- **No, she doesn't**.

This tense is used to express facts:

- Tom **works** at Lowis Engineering in London but he **lives** in Croydon.
- The office **is** on the corner of Wardour Street and Oxford Street.
- Diane **works** in London but she comes from the USA.

and for actions that are regular activities or routines:

- I **check** my emails every day.
- The mailman **brings** the mail before lunch.

It is also used with timetables and schedules:

- The cafeteria **opens** at 12 o'clock.
- The company **closes** at midnight.

Words that often take the present simple are: *often, seldom, usually, never, always, normally, rarely*:

- It **often rains** a lot in April.
- We **never close**.

Exercise 3

Complete the questions and answers with the present simple form of the verb in parentheses.

1 Where _____ you _____ from? (come)

2 I _____ from Venice. (come)

3   Who _____ you _____ for? (work)
4   I _____ for an electronics company. (work)
5   What time _____ your boss _____ in the office? (arrive)
6   She usually _____ to the office at about eight o'clock. (get)
7   How often _____ she _____ on vacation? (go)
8   She never _____ any vacation at all! (take)

Going to future

Positive forms:

- I'm [I am] going to send an email tomorrow.
- They're [They are] going to complain about the meeting.
- He's [He is] going to book three conference rooms.
- We're going to write to the manager.

Negative forms:

- I'm not [I am not] going to telephone tomorrow.
- We aren't [We are not] going to eat in the restaurant tonight.
- She isn't going to go to Australia.

Questions:

- Are you going to telephone tomorrow?
- Is he going to tell the boss?
- Who's going to tell the boss?

Long answers:

- Yes, I'm going to telephone tomorrow.
- No, I'm not going to telephone tomorrow.
- Yes, they're going to email the manager.
- No, they aren't going to email the manager.

Short answers:

- Yes, I am.
- No, I'm not.
- Yes, he is.
- No, he isn't.
- Yes, they are.
- No, they aren't.

This tense is used if we believe something is going to happen:

- We**'re going to** move offices next year.
- When **are** you **going to** get a company car?
- When I get home, I**'m going to** write a report about the conference.

Exercise 4

Complete the sentences with the words in the box.

I'm	is	isn't	going	not	to

1 When I get to the office, _____ going to have a meeting with Robert.
2 Next summer we're _____ to spend some time sailing in the Mediterranean.
3 _____ he going to come to the conference?
4 John and Karen phoned. They aren't going _____ be here on time.
5 _____ Robert going to finish the integration by the end of December? I don't think so!

Past simple

Positive forms:

- He **arrived** yesterday.
- I **cancelled** my meeting last week.
- We **visited** the company last month.
- She **knew** there was a delay.
- We **ate** in the restaurant last night.

Negatives and questions are formed with *did*:

- He **didn't [did not] telephone** yesterday.
- You **didn't tell** me that she was here.
- They **didn't enjoy** their visit.
- I **didn't expect** to wait so long at reception.
- **Did** Mr. Lawson **arrive** yesterday?
- **Did** you **enjoy** your visit?
- **Did** the suppliers **receive** their money?
- What **did** you **buy** in London?

Long answers:

- Yes, he **arrived** yesterday.
- No, he **didn't arrive** yesterday.
- Yes, we **spoke** to the manager about your problem.
- No, we **didn't speak** to the manager about your problem.

Short answers:

- Yes, we **did**.
- No, we **didn't**.
- Yes, I **did**.
- No, I **didn't**.

The past simple is used for finished actions in the past. They can be a long time ago or very recent:

- I **visited** your company last week.
- Columbus **sailed** to America in 1492.

Words that often take the past simple are: *yesterday, an hour ago, last year, in 2009, last week, a year ago.*

Exercise 5

Complete the sentence with the correct past simple form (positive, negative, question) of the verb in parentheses.

1   I _____ the report before I went home. (finish)
2   She _____ to me after the meeting. (not speak)
3   _____ Tom _____ Karen yesterday evening? (telephone)
4   What _____ Diane _____ about the problem? (do)
5   They _____ me the report on time. (not email)
6   I _____ a meeting last night with John. (have)

Simple future – *will*

Positive forms:

- I'll [I **will**] **mail** it tomorrow.
- We'll **arrange** a meeting.
- Tom'll **call me** as soon as your taxi is here.

Negative forms:

- I **won't** [will not] **do** it tomorrow.
- John **won't forget** to do it, Karen.
- They **won't come** back.

Questions:

- **Will** you **do** it tomorrow?
- **Will** she **call** me a taxi?
- When **will** my taxi **come**?

Long answers:

- Yes, I'**ll do** it in a minute.
- No, **I won't do** it today.

Short answers:

- Yes, **I will**.
- No, **I won't**.

This tense is used for predictions about the future:

- In the year 2020 we'**ll** all work until we are 75.
- You'**ll** never finish that report before 1:00.

It is also used to give information about the future (that does not involve intentions or arrangements):

- In ten minutes we'**ll test** the fire alarm.

It must also be used for conditional use, for example in *if*-sentences:

- If you **do not cancel** in time, you'll have to pay a fee.

It is also used to announce a decision in offers, promises and threats, requests and instructions, and suggestions:

- That sounds good. I'**ll have** the steak too.
- I'**ll tell** you as soon as the report is ready.
- I promise I'**ll inform** my boss immediately.
- Do that again and I'**ll complain** to your boss.
- **Will** you **fill in** this form, please?

Exercise 6

Match the sentences from different conversations.

1	Can I speak to Catherine, please?	A I'll find a new job!
2	You were fired! What'll you do now?	B Don't worry, I'll send it again.
3	When can we have lunch?	C Oh yes. I'll probably see them after lunch.
4	Will you see Tony and Andrea today?	D You're right. I'll speak to the boss about the problem.
5	I can't find the report you emailed me.	E Of course. I'll get her.
6	We don't have enough people!	F Wait a moment and I'll check my calendar.

Phrasal verbs

- I must **call up** Robert.
- Can you **put** me **through to** John?

- **Hold on** and I'll (I will) connect you.
- Don't **put down** the receiver.
- John **picked up** the receiver when the phone rang.
- Can you **fill in** the form?
- 2,000 workers were **laid off** by the company.
- He **got up** at six o'clock in the morning.

A phrasal verb is a combination of a verb *(call, put, hold)* and a word like *down, up, through*. With many phrasal verbs we can separate the two parts.

- Karen can **pick** Tom **up** from the airport.
- Kim **put** the cup of coffee **down** on the table.

Here are some more useful examples with their meaning. Keep a note of any phrasal verbs you see and add them to this list.

- back up – make a copy of something
- set up – start a business
- close down – stop a business
- cut off – disconnect
- hold up – cause a delay
- turn on / off – start / stop a piece of electrical equipment

Prepositions of time

- The meeting is **at** ten o'clock.
- We close the office **at** Christmas time.
- I'm meeting Karen **at** lunchtime / the weekend [UK] / night.
- The next conference is **in** June.
- The company was founded **in** 1981.
- We need to organize a team-building exercise **in** the spring.
- China is going to be the most powerful economy **in** the 21st century.
- We had tea **in** the afternoon.
- I saw him **on** Wednesday.
- She sent me the email **on** Friday afternoon.
- I'm flying back to London **on** New Years Eve.
- The new offices were opened **on** Monday July 21st.
- I usually play tennis **on** the weekends. [US]

We use *at, on* and *in* with these time expressions.

at – particular times, festival times and specific fixed expressions
in – months, years, seasons, centuries, parts of the day
on – days of the week, parts of named days, festival days, dates

Exercise 7

Complete the sentences with *at*, *in* or *on*.

1 John and Karen are flying _____ Sunday morning to London.
2 APU bought Lowis Engineering _____ 2012.
3 We have a meeting with the lawyers _____ 10.30.
4 APU plans to roll out the new software _____ the summer.
5 I received the report _____ Christmas day.
6 The workshops take place _____ the weekend. [UK]

How much / many / a little / a few

* How **much time** do we have?
* Do you have **many offices** in Asia?
* I don't have **much coffee**.
* The company doesn't have **many servers**.
* He only has **a little money** in the bank.
* They have **a few people** in New York.
* There are only **a few salespeople**.

We use *many* and a *few* for nouns we can count, for example *people, offices, chairs*, and *much* and *a little* for nouns we cannot count, for example *money, time, space, water, information, capacity*. Much / many are normally used with questions and negatives.

Exercise 8

Underline the correct word in the sentences.

1 He isn't paying *many / much* money for the information.
2 Britain doesn't have *much /many* mountains.
3 We only interviewed *a few / a little* colleagues about the problem.
4 How *much / many* factories does the company have in Ukraine?
5 There's only *a few / a little* water in the cooling system.
6 How *much / many* luggage does she have?

Modals for obligation: *must, have to, mustn't, don't have to*

Positive forms:

* **I must speak** to my boss.
* **I have to fly** to Sydney.
* Karen **has to take** a taxi to the station.
* We **must have** a meeting about this.

We use these modal verbs to show there is some kind of obligation or necessity to do something.

We use *must* for strong personal obligations or strong personal advice.

- I **must telephone** my mother this evening.

We use *have to* where an external rule or situation creates an obligation.

- The bad weather means we **have to cancel** the picnic.

Negative forms:

- You **mustn't (must not) speak** to him about this.
- She **doesn't (does not) have** to come to work tomorrow.
- I **mustn't (must not) forget** to book a hotel room.

We can use *must not* to say something is not allowed.

- You **mustn't (must not) smoke** in the office.

But the negative form of *don't have to* means there is no necessity to do something.

- I **don't have to wear** a tie in the office.

Question forms:

- **Do** we **have to** send the report by Friday?
- **Does** he **have to check** the documents again?
- What **do** they **have to do** next?

Long answers:

- Yes, we **have to**.
- No, we **don't have to send** it by then.

Short answers:

- Yes, we **do**. / No, we **don't**.

Exercise 9

Complete the sentences with *must, have to, mustn't or don't have to*.

1 Our accountant says we _____ pay our taxes this week.
2 We _____ go to lunch some time soon.
3 Why do we _____ take a plane? We can go by train.
4 If you want to drive home after the party, then you really _____ drink any alcohol.
5 The boss says we _____ meet him in his office in ten minutes.
6 I'm not feeling well. I _____ finish the report today, so I'm going home.

Comparison of adjectives

We use comparative adjectives to compare two things.
One-syllable adjective add –er.
Rich → richer
Adjectives ending in –y change to –ier.
Lazy → lazier
Adjectives with two or more syllables have *more / less* before the adjective
Difficult → more / less difficult
Comparisons are often made using *than*.

*   The Pacific is larger than the Atlantic

Watch out!

Some adjectives have irregular comparative forms:
good → better
bad → worse
far → further / farther
big→ bigger

Exercise 10

Complete the sentence with the correct comparative form of the adjective in parentheses.

1   I don't like this job. It's _____ (hard) than I thought it would be.
2   Diane said the restaurant was _____ (good) than the cafeteria.
3   I want to take the train instead of flying because it's _____ (cheap).
4   I need some pills. My headache is much _____ (bad) now.
5   Everybody is _____ (happy) now that we've moved offices.
6   This project is _____ (difficult) than we expected

Superlatives

We use superlative forms to compare one member of a group with the whole group. **Short (one syllable)** adjectives add *the +-est* in the superlative form.

*   Germany has **the largest economy** in Europe.

Longer adjectives add *the most / the least* before the adjective.

*   The Ritz is **the most expensive hotel** in London.

We decided to travel by bus. It was **the least expensive** option.

Irregular forms:
Some common adjectives have irregular superlative forms:
good→ the best
bad→ the worst

far→ the farthest / furthest
big→ the biggest

Exercise 11

Complete the sentence with the correct superlative form of the adjective in parentheses.

1 London is _____ (big) city in the European Union.
2 My flight was delayed by 24 hours. It was _____ (bad) delay I've ever had.
3 We cancelled the contract. It was _____ (good) decision in the situation.
4 Diane took the train to Paris from London. It was _____ (fast) option.
5 We decided to use the Hotel Orbis for our conference. It was _____ (suitable) hotel.
6 This building is _____ (expensive) our company has built.

First conditional

Positive forms:

- If **I see** Mr. Field, **I'll (I will) give** him the message.
- If he**'s** (he **is**) in the office, he**'ll** (he **will**) **call** you.
- If they**'re** (they **are**) late, they**'ll** (they **will**) **miss** their flight.

Negative form:

- If it **isn't** (**is not**) ready, she**'ll** (she **will**) come later.

Questions:

- What**'ll** (what **will**) you do if the train **is cancelled**?
- **Will** she **be able to see** me if I come to the office?

Long answers:

- I**'ll** (I **will**) **take** a taxi.

Short answers:

- Yes, you **will**.
- No, you **won't** (**will not**).

Conditional sentences have two parts or clauses: the condition (*if*) clause and the result clause. We use the first conditional to talk about conditions that are probable or expected in the future:

- If the train is late, we**'ll take** a taxi.

We use the present simple in the *if* clause and *will / won't* + the infinitive in the result clause. The clauses can come in either order. If the result clause is first, there is no comma:

- We**'ll telephone** Diane if we **have** time.
- If we **have** time, we**'ll telephone** Diane.

Exercise 12

Join the two parts of the sentence together.

1	If the weather's good,	A	the drive will take about twenty minutes.
2	We'll come to the meeting	B	if I offer more money?
3	If the roads are clear,	C	we'll work outside.
4	What'll he do	D	if there aren't enough people.
5	We'll have a problem	E	if you arrange a meeting room.

Can for ability

We use *can* and *can't* to talk about our ability to do something, either at this moment or in general.

- **Can** you **play** golf? (= Do you have the skills?)
- **Can** you all **see** the slide? (= Is it possible for you to see it?)

We also use *can* to say that we have permission to do something.

- You **can drive** a car when you're seventeen.
- You **can't eat** food in here.
- He **can sleep** in the living room.

The past form is *could*.

- My daughter **could speak** three languages when she was five.
- I **couldn't** (could not) **understand** anything they said.

***Will be able to* is used for future ability.**

- The new BMW electric car **will be able to drive** at 120 km/h.

Exercise 13

Complete the sentences with the words in the box. You may have to use them more than once.

able	be	can	can't	couldn't

1   My grandmother _____ speak Mandarin perfectly, but she _____ write it.
2   We'll go on the train so we'll be _____ to work together on our way to the meeting.
3   He _____ fly to Boston yesterday because of bad weather.
4   _____ you telephone me in about ten minutes?
5   You _____ sit in here. It's reserved for women only.
6   The Russian spacecraft is so fast it'll _____ able to reach Mars in only a month.

Should / shouldn't / ought to for recommendations

Positive forms:

- You **should see** a doctor.
- She **ought to telephone** him.
- They **should hire** a consultant.

Negative forms:

- We **shouldn't (should not) wait** too long.
- They **shouldn't (should not) have borrowed** any money.

Question form:

- Do you think he **should do** that?
- What do you think I **ought to do**?

We use *should / ought to* to give advice or an opinion. They have the same meaning but *should* is more common.
We use *should have / ought to have* when we want to talk about the past.

- You **should have gone** to the meeting.
- We **ought to have paid** the money on time.
- I **shouldn't (should not) have talked** to him about it.

Exercise 14

Join the two parts of the sentence together.

1	You shouldn't	A	known about the strike.
2	We ought to talk	B	bought the building.
3	They should have	C	smoke. It's bad for you.
4	He ought to	D	say in the meeting?
5	They shouldn't have	E	to the supplier about the problem.
6	What should she	F	find a new job.

Time phrases

- She'll give you her address **when** she calls.
- I'll help you **after** I finish this report.
- We'll start the meeting **as soon as** the boss arrives.
- We won't wait **until** Paul gets here.

Will is not used after the words *if, when, until, as soon as* and *after*. With these time phrases we use the present simple with the time phrase and *will* in the main clause. If the time phrase is at the beginning of the sentence, we put a comma before the main clause.

- **As soon as I get** to the office, **I'll send** an email.
- **I'll send** an email **as soon as I get** to the office.

Exercise 15

Complete the sentences with the words in the box.

finished	is	soon	until	wait

1   When the report _____ ready, I'll read it.
2   Karen will start the meeting as _____ as John arrives.
4   After the project is _____, Lowis Engineering will be integrated into APU.
5   I won't start _____ the report arrives.
6   If Diane is late, we'll _____.

Present perfect simple

Positive forms:

- I've [I have] **worked here** for ten years.
- She's [She has] **done** secretarial work for ten years.
- The manager **has read** your letter.

Negative forms:

- I **haven't** [have not] **worked** in an office before.
- She hasn't [has not] **called** a taxi.

Questions:

- **Have** you **worked** in London before?
- **Has** my taxi **been called**?
- Where **have** you **put** the brochures?

Long answers:

- Yes, I've **worked** in London for five years.
- No, I **haven't** [have not] **called** a taxi.

Short answers:

- Yes, I **have**.
- No, I **haven't**.
- Yes, it **has**.
- No, it **hasn't**.

The present perfect simple is formed with *have* + the past participle (see page XYZ for irregular verbs). It is used to describe a completed action in the past which is still relevant to the present.

- Can you help me? I've **lost** the key to my office. (= I don't have it.)
- We **have to cancel** our visit because she's broken her leg. (= Her leg is broken.)

- I've read some information about your company. (= I know about the company.)
- We**'ve moved** offices since your last visit. (= The offices are different.)

Note that we do not use the present perfect if we say when something happened, for example, with finished time expressions such as *yesterday, last week, at 10 o'clock this morning, in 2010, last October*.

- I'm sure we**'ve met** before!
- **Have** you ever **visited** APU before?
- My boss **has been** to a conference here.
- The company **has been** in the APU Group for over 25 years.

It is also used to describe events with expressions of 'time passing up to now'. Signal words are *just, yet, already.*

- **Have** you **sent** the report yet?
- She**'s** just **finished** the email.
- We**'ve** already **had** some meetings with APU.

We use the present perfect to give news.

- APU **has bought** Lowis Engineering. (= The date is not important.)

Exercise 16

Put the words in the sentences into the correct order.

1 York / you / to / ever / Have / been / New?
2 hasn't / contract / signed / She / the.
3 moved / We've / again / offices.
4 contract / company / Sunstone / has / won / The / the.
5 already / to / sent / finished / I've / the / my / report / and / it / boss.
6 he / yet / answered / email / Has / your?

---

too and *not ... either*

- 'I drive a Mercedes'. 'Oh, me **too**!'
- 'We want to go on the Queen Mary II to New York.' 'We do **too**.'
- 'The email system **isn't** (**is not**) **working**.' 'I know. And the Internet **isn't working** either.'

When we have the same experience as another person we can use *too* for positive forms or *not ... either* for negative forms.

Exercise 17

Match the sentences from different conversations.

1 I hate this software!   A Yes, and he's often bad-tempered too.
2 We need to have a meeting about this.   B I don't like it either.
3 John seems very tired.   C No, and not tomorrow either.

4   Will you see Diane today?
5   I can't find the email John sent.
6   I really like his car!

D   You're quite right. I think so too.
E   I do too. It's so fast.
F   I can't find it either!

Adverbs

slow → slowly
intelligent → intelligently
cheap→ cheaply

We use adverbs to describe *how* something happens:

*   The team worked **quickly**.
*   We make regular adverbs by adding *–ly* to an adjective or *–ily* to an adjective ending in *y*.
*   The photocopier prints **quickly**.
*   The man fell **heavily** to the ground.

Adverbs of frequency like *always*, *often*, *never* usually come before the main part of the verb, but after the verb *to be*:

*   James is **always** late.

We can put many adverbs after the verb and its object:

*   Kim sings **beautifully**.
*   Petra closed the window **quietly**.

Irregular forms:

Adjectives ending in *–ly* (*lonely*, *lovely*, *friendly*) do not need to be changed

*   She looks **lovely**.

Some words are both adjectives and adverbs:

*   He's a **fast** driver; he drives **fast**.
*   Tim has a **hard** job; he has to work **hard**.
*   The plane was **late**; it landed **late**.
*   My boss was at work early; he arrived early.

The adverb from good is *well*:

*   Hong is a good worker. She works **well**.

Exercise 18

Change the adjective into an adverb in the sentences below.

1   I shut down my computer _____ (quick) and left the office.
2   She drove home _____ (slow) in the dark.

3 The report was sent _____ (early) in the morning.
4 My meeting was cancelled _____ (sudden) because of illness.
5 The server works extremely _____ (fast).
6 This new program helps us deal with the problems _____ (intelligent).

Passives

Positive forms:

- These shoes **are made** in Italy.
- Safety helmets **must be worn** at all times.
- The work **will be finished** on time.
- The meeting **was cancelled**.

Negative form:

- The reports **aren't (are not) sent** to headquarters.

We use the active form to talk about who or what did something:

- Diane **called** John Carter.

Sometimes this subject or 'agent' is not very important, or not known, but we still want to know what happens. In this case we can use the passive.

The signal **is sent** every five minutes.

We form the passive with the appropriate form of the verb be **+ the past participle. It is often used in writing for reports, to describe processes and formal notices. If we want to mention the agent, we use** by.

- The employees **are trained by** Karen Armstrong.
- The engine **is cooled with** water.

Exercise 19

Put the words in the sentences into the correct order.
1 conference / cancelled / last / The / was / week.
2 package / courier / by / will / The / be / sent.
3 management / are / reports / read / by / the / Her / top.
4 temperature / five / The / checked / minutes / is / every.
5 I / be / driven / airport / to / must / the.
6 with / house / The / is / solar / heated / power.

Unit 1   Back in the office

Conversation

1   Diane wants Tom to come to a meeting with John Carter and Karen Taylor from APU.

See page 8 for video script.

Understanding

2

1   Yes, he does. Tom knows Cathy and Julia.
2   Yes, he did. Tom enjoyed his weekend.
3   Jasmine is making photocopies for Tom.
4   Tom is changing the agenda.
5   Cathy telephones Tom.
6   They will meet John Carter and Karen Taylor in the board room.

Practice

3

1   C   2   E   3   D   4   B   5   A

4

1   Hello! / Hi!
2   Good weekend?
3   How was your weekend?
4   Good morning!
5   How are you?

5

Tom	Morning, Roberta.
Roberta	Morning, Tom. How are you?
Tom	Fine, thanks. Good weekend?
Roberta	Great, thanks. I played golf on Sunday. How was your weekend?
Tom	Very nice, thanks.

6
See page 11 for audio script.

Speaking

7

Model conversation

Colin	Morning!
You	*Morning, Colin!*
Colin	How are you?
You	*Fine, thanks, and you?*
Colin	Very well, thanks. Good weekend?
You	*Great thanks! How was your vacation?*
Colin	Very good, thanks. We went to France. What are you working on at the moment?
You	*Oh, I'm practising my English.*
Colin	That's a good idea!
You	*What are you doing?*
Colin	Oh, I'm waiting for some coffee.

Unit 2 Visitors to the company

Conversation

1 Diane hasn't met Karen Taylor before.

See page 12 for video script.

Understanding

2

1 A   2 C   3 B

Practice

3

1 E   2 D   3 A   4 C   5 B

4

1 to / too
2 of / at
3 for
4 to
5 in

5

Jasmine	Hi, John, good to see you again!
John	Hello, Jasmine, good to see you again, too.
Jasmine	Can I introduce my colleague, Julia?
John	Pleased to meet you.
Julia	Pleased to meet you, too.
John	What do you do, Julia?
Julia	I'm Mr Fisher's personal assistant.

6

See page 15 for audio script.

Speaking

7

Model conversation

You	Jenny! Good to see you again!
Jenny	Oh, hello! Good to see you again too! Can I introduce my colleague, Alex?
You	Hello, Alex, nice to meet you!
Alex	Nice to meet you too.
You	What do you do, Alex?
Alex	Oh I'm responsible for sales and marketing. What about you?
You	I'm a sales manager.
Alex	Interesting.
You	Let me introduce you to my colleague, Tom.
Jenny, Alex, Tom	Hi ... hello ... pleased to meet you both.
You	Let me give you my card.
Alex:	Oh, thanks. Here's mine!

Unit 3   Down to business

Conversation

1   Tom is going to help Karen from APU with integrating Lowis into APU.

See page 16 for video script.

Understanding

2

1   True.
2   False, she deal with systems.
3   True.
4   False, Karen does want Tom's help.
5   True.
6   False, John does want to make a phone call.

Practice

3

1   would
2   mind
3   need
4   coming
5   Could
6   by

4

1   Would you mind if we open the windows?
2   The boss really needs you to give him a call.
3   Let's start by checking some information.
4   She'd like you to come to the meeting.
5   Could you check my reservation?
6   Thank you all for coming to this meeting this morning.

5

Sample answers

1   James, I want you to do something for me.

2   Would you mind if I turn on the light?
3   Could you give me some paper?
4   The company really needs you to help me with this project.
5   When that's finished, I'd like you to join my team.

Speaking

6

See page 19 for audio script.

7

Model conversation

You	OK, thank you for coming to this meeting.
Helen + Colin	OK, good.
You	Now, I really need you to do some things for me.
Helen + Colin	Fine. No problem.
You	Colin, could you check the project costs for me?
Colin	Sure. Can I get the figures from you tomorrow morning?
You	I'm not going to be in the office tomorrow morning. Can you come to my office after the meeting?
Colin	Of course.
You	Helen, I'd like you to visit the factory with me.
Helen	Great! When?
You	I'm going to check it on Monday next week.
Helen	OK.
You	Finally, could you send me all your reports by Friday lunch time?
Helen + Colin	Sure. No problem.

Unit 4   The presentation

Conversation

1 France [Strasbourg], Korea [Seoul] and the USA [Houston]

See page 20 for video script.

Understanding

2

1 C   2 A   3 B

Practice

3

1 D   2 A   3 B   4 C

4

1 like
2 firstly
3 secondly
4 all
5 After
6 then

5

Suggested answers

1 I would like to tell you something about my company.
2 Firstly, the size.
3 Secondly, the products.
4 So first of all, we have offices in more than 50 countries and 200,000 people work for us.
5 After we opened offices in Korea in 2008, we then built factories in Vietnam.

6

See page 23 for audio script.

Speaking

7

Model presentation

> I'd like to tell you about the new payment terms, first the change in terms and second the reasons for the change.
>
> So, first of all, the change in terms. From January 1st the payment terms will be 90 days not 60 days.
>
> Second, the reason for the change in terms. Ninety days is what our customers require.

Unit 5 Questions and answers at the presentation

Conversation

1 Diane was a sales manager, responsible for Asia.

See page 24 for video script.

Understanding

2

1 False, she worked in Seoul, too.
2 True
3 False, Lee Ji-Sung was responsible for the xRoot project in Asia.
4 True
5 False, he says it went fast.

Practice

3

1 glad
2 understand
3 good
4 I
5 me

4

1 Do you have any questions about the presentation?
2 I'm not sure about that point.
3 Let me think about that question.
4 Thank you for asking that question.

5

Suggested answers

1 Do you have any questions?
2 Sorry, I don't understand your question.
3 I'm not sure about that.
4 Let me think

Speaking

6

See page 26 for audio script.

7

Model conversation

You	Do you have any questions?
C1	Yes. How much time did you need to develop your product?
You	Sorry, I don't understand your question.
C1	I mean, how long did it take from start to finish?
You	I see. It took nine months.
C2	Was the product tested in Taiwan?
You	I'm not quite sure about that. Can I send you the answer by email?
C2	Of course. How many people worked on the project?
You	I'm glad you asked that question. It wasn't many, only six engineers.

8

Model conversation

You	Were you responsible for the project?
Supplier	Yes, I was.
You	How much did the project cost?
Supplier	I'm afraid I can't tell you that information.
You	I understand. Where did the six engineers work?
Supplier	They worked as a team in the UK.
You	Thanks. That's all.
Supplier	My pleasure.

Unit 6   Closing the meeting

Conversation

1   Tom promises to send Karen a list of the IT systems in Lowis.

See page 28 for video script.

Understanding

2

1   Tom and Karen will work on the integration project ~~part time~~. *full time*

2   John and Diane will have a meeting every ~~month~~. *week*

3   On ~~Friday~~ Tom will send the list of IT systems to Karen. *Wednesday*

4   Diane ordered some ~~pizzas~~ for lunch. *sandwiches*

5   Karen doesn't eat ~~fruit~~. *meat*

Practice

3

1   C   2   A   3   B   4   E   5   D

4

1   I think that's enough for today.

2   Please help yourself to something to eat.

3   Could you pass me some orange juice, John?

4   Would you like some fruit?

5

Suggested answers

1   Could you pass me a [bottle of] mineral water?

2   Are you OK with that?

3   Would you like some cheese?

4   I'm afraid I don't eat meat.

5   Have some mango. It's delicious!

6

See page 31 for audio script.

Speaking

7

Model conversation

You	*I think that's enough for today.*
Cindy	That's good.
You	*So, I ordered some refreshments. I hope you're hungry!*
Cindy	Yes. Very.
You	*Please help yourself!*
Cindy	Mm, it looks great!
You	*Could you pass me an orange juice, please?*
Cindy	Here you are. Um … is that beef in the sandwich? I'm afraid I don't eat meat!
You	*Would you like a cheese salad sandwich?*
Cindy	Oh, thanks! Sorry to be difficult!
You	*No problem. I can't eat fish myself.*

Unit 7   On the phone to Australia

Telephone call

1   Karen is on a business trip.

See page 32 for video script.

Understanding

2

1 C   **2** B   **3** C   **4** A

Practice

3

1 E   **2** A   **3** B   **4** C   **5** D

4

1   Can you put me through to Julia, please?

2   I'm afraid he's in a meeting at the moment.

3   Can I speak to Jasmine Goodman, please?

4   I'll write him an email.

5   Hi, this is David Knopf from xRoot Software.

5

Suggested answers

1   (Your name) speaking.

2   I'm afraid he / she is in a meeting.

3   Hold the line, please.

4   I'm sorry but his line's busy

5   Can I take a message?

6

See page 35 for audio script.

Speaking

7

Model conversation

Jodie	Compex Incorporated, Jodie King speaking. How can I help you?
You	*Hello, this Michelle Blanc from Tapette. Can I speak to Frank Linker, please?*
Jodie	I'm afraid he's in a meeting.
You	*OK. I'll send him an email. Could you put me through to Susie Goh?*
Jodie	I'm sorry but her line's busy at the moment. Can I take a message?
You	*Don't worry, I'll call back later. Thank you very much for your assistance. Goodbye!*
Jodie	Goodbye!

Unit 8   Emailing Australia

Email

1 Tom suggests a telephone conference call.

Understanding

2

1 False, he emailed her. He spoke to Kim.

2 False, she is on a business trip.

3 False, Tom wants to organize a telephone conference.

4 False, she is back in the office on Friday.

5 True.

Practice

3

1 With regard to **your** project in India … .

2 I think it's **a** good idea if we … .

3 I tried to speak to you this morning **but** you were in a meeting.

4 I suggest that **we** meet as soon as possible.

5 Could you let **me** know if that's convenient?

6 I'm out of the office **until** Monday.

4

> Dear Ms Goodman
>
> I tried to call you this afternoon but you were in a meeting.
>
> With regard to our meeting tomorrow, I think it's a good idea if we also discuss the project costs. I suggest that I invite our accountant, Gordon King, to the meeting.

> I look forward to seeing you tomorrow.
>
> Best wishes
>
> Priti Makesch

5

Suggested answers

1 Bernhard

2 this morning

3 visiting a customer

4 project

5 visit you next week

6 bring my colleague

7 James

Writing

6

Model email

> Dear Amy
>
> I tried to return your call but I heard you are flying to China.
>
> With regard to your questions, I think it's a good idea if we speak on the phone. I suggest I call you tomorrow at 6pm Beijing time. Can you send me the telephone number of the hotel?
>
> I look forward to speaking to you tomorrow.
>
> Best wishes
>
> Pascale

7

Model out-of-office message

> I am away from Model out-of-office message _____ to _____ on vacation. Please contact Susan Smith on smith@XYZ.com with any enquiries.

Unit 9 Starting the telephone conference call

Telephone conference call

1 Tom is at home.

See page 40 for audio script.

Understanding

2

1 Tom is working from home today.
2 Because it is an international company and needs different systems for different countries.
3 It only takes two days.

Practice

3

1	F	2	C	3	G	4	E
5	B	6	D	7	A		

4

1 Diane works from home on Mondays.
2 I'm sitting here with Kim and Bernadette.
3 Can you tell me how much it costs?
4 Do you know how many offices you have worldwide?

5

John	John Carter here. Hello, Mr Park.
Mr Park	Good evening, Mr Carter.
John	My colleague Karen Taylor will call in in a moment from home.
Karen	Hello John, hello Mr Park. Sorry I'm late.
Mr Park	No problem, Ms Taylor.

John	Good. Well, let's start. Can you tell us how much time you have for us today?
Mr Park	As much time as you want, Mr Carter.
John	Great! Well, first of all, we need to know how much your new products will cost?

Speaking

6

See page 43 for audio script.

7

Model conversation

Recorded voice	Another caller is entering the conference.
You	*Hello, it's Paul here.*
Jun + Pascale	Hi, Jun here. Hello, this is Pascale!
You	*Hi there. Sorry I'm late.*
Pascale	That's OK!
You	*I'm working from home today. How much time do we need?*
Jun	As much time as you want. Well, let's start. Can you tell us how many people you have for this project in your office?
You	*Not many, only a few. How many people do you have, Pascale?*
Pascale	Oh it's the same for me. Only a few.
You	*Can you tell me how many people you need?*
Pascale	I think another five at least!

Unit 10   Ending the telephone conference call

Telephone conference call

1   Tom is staying one night in Portsmouth.

See page 44 for video script.

Understanding

2

1   False, Karen is flying to London next week.

2   True

3   False, Tom is visiting a customer, not a supplier.

4   False, He says he's not sure if that's a really good idea.

5   True

Practice

3

1   Speak

2   lunchtime

3   Mr Carter's

4   seeing

5   Tuesday

4

1   D   2   A   3   B   4   C

5

1	John	I just want to let you know. I'm flying to Seoul last week. *next*
2	Mr Park	Oh, let my check my schedule. *me*
3	John:	How do Wednesday look? *does*
4	Mr Park	Hmm, not too bad. What about on 10 o'clock in your hotel? *at*

5	John	That's fine. I'm have a meeting at the APU office after lunch. *having*
6	Mr Park	OK. So, 10 o'clock Wednesday. Nice speaking at you, John. *to*
7	John	Yes. He's looking forward to seeing you soon! *I'm*

Speaking

6

See page 47 for audio script.

7

Model conversation

Jun	Well, I think ...and I think a meeting is a very good idea.
You	*I'm flying to Tokyo next week.*
Jun	Let me check my schedule.
You	*How does Tuesday afternoon look?*
Jun	Oh, I'm sorry, I'm visiting a supplier outside Tokyo on Tuesday.
You	*Well, I'm staying in Tokyo until Friday.*
Jun	Oh, very good. Then I have a chance to see you on Thursday morning.
You	*Hmm, I'm meeting somebody at my hotel in the morning. What about your plans for Thursday afternoon?*
Jun	Yes, that's fine. Is three o'clock OK?
You	*That's an excellent idea.*
Jun	Great. Well, it was good to speak to you, Karl. See you next week!
You	*I'm looking forward to it, Jun. Goodbye.*
Jun	Goodbye!

Unit 11   Making plans by email

Email

1 Karen suggests that she comes to Tom's meeting on Monday morning with the Lowis sales team.

Understanding

2

1 Karen wants to come to Tom's meeting.

2 The sales people don't use the APU system yet.

3 Tom and Karen are driving to Portsmouth.

4 Karen must meet Peter King on Tuesday morning.

5 Karen has to check the servers for John.

6 Karen has to fly back to Sydney on Friday.

Practice

3

1 E   **2** C   **3** B   **4** A   **5** D

4

1 Would you mind speaking to Jun and Pascale?

2 What's your opinion on the problem?

3 Do you think you could send me the report?

4 Shall we send the figures to the project manager?

5 If this is OK for you, we can work together.

6 Why don't we have a meeting on Wednesday?

5

1 Why don't

2 we could

3 do you feel about this

4 this is OK with

5 must

6 you mind

Writing

6

Model email

Dear Pascale

I'm visiting Paris next week for a sales conference. Why don't we have a meeting to discuss the project progress? If you're OK with this, perhaps we could go for lunch. How do you feel about this?

Shall we meet at your office at one o'clock? Would you mind making reservations in a restaurant?

Best regards

Jun

Unit 12 Telephone small talk

Telephone call

1 John's suggestion is that Tom visit Australia for a week.

See page 52 for audio script.

Understanding

2

1 A **2** B **3** C

Practice

3

1 What are ... .
2 I have to check ... .
3 Did you ... .
4 I was wondering if you ... .
5 When is a good ... .

4

1 It's raining here.
2 What are you doing this evening?
3 What's work like at the moment?
4 Did you see the football last night?
5 When is a good time for you?

5

Karen	How's the weather in London?
Peter	It's raining here.
Karen	Too bad! Listen, I'm visiting the UK next week. I was wondering if we could have a meeting some time?
Peter	Well, on Tuesday perhaps.
Karen	Sure. When's a good time for you? The afternoon maybe?
Peter	Hmm, I have to check my schedule. Oh, I'm sorry but the afternoon's no good.
Karen	Well, what are you doing on Tuesday morning?
Peter	Tuesday morning is fine.

Speaking

6

See page 55 for audio script.

7

Model conversation

You	*Hello, Colin. How's the weather?*
Colin	Oh, hello! It's raining here!
You	*Too bad! What's work like at the moment?*
Colin	Very busy!
You	*I'm visiting Manchester next week. I was wondering if I could visit you.*
Colin	Well, next week is busy, but I'm sure it's possible.
You	*What are your plans for Thursday?*
Colin	Hmm, not so good. What are you doing on Wednesday?
You	*I have to check my schedule.*
Colin	No problem.
You	*When is a good time for you on Wednesday?*
Colin	Wednesday morning is fine.

Unit 13 Arranging the business trip

Email

1 He plans to stay eight nights.

Understanding

2

1 Tom wants APU to book a hotel room for him.

2 Tom suggests a telephone conference and inviting Robert Holden and Peter King to the telco.

3 John thinks a telco is a good idea but that it is not necessary to invite Robert Holden and Peter King.

4 Pia Levene, John's assistant, will arrange the hotel room.

5 To do something on the Saturday night.

Practice

3

1 for	**2** if	**3** As	
4 for	**5** ending		

4

1 Let me know if that date is OK.

2 The week ending 25 June is good for me.

3 Following our meeting this afternoon, here are my notes.

4 Thanks for your phone call this morning.

5 Would it be possible for you to reserve a meeting room?

5

1 following – Following

2 Febuary - February

3 bee – be

4 arrives – arrive / will arrive

5 regard – regards

6 late – let

7 best – Best

Writing

6

Model email

> Dear Mr Murray
>
> Thank you for your email yesterday. I think your services sound very interesting. Would it be possible for you to visit my office next month on 12 June?
>
> If you want, my assistant will reserve a hotel for you.
>
> Please let me know if this is possible.
>
> Best regards
>
> ...

7

Model email

> Dear ...
>
> Thank you very much for your reply to my email. 12 June in the morning is good for me. What time would you like to meet? Thanks for your offer to reserve a hotel room but that is not necessary.

Unit 14   Priorities for the business trip

Email

1   Karen is the first person on the conference call.

See page 60 for audio script.

Understanding

2
1   data centre
2   data security
3   developments
4   accounting
5   important

Practice

3
1   D   2   A   3   B   4   C

4
1   that
2   to
3   second / secondly
4   of
5   important

5
(Example answers)
1   check your emails
2   plan your schedule
3   answer your emails
4   go to lunch!

6
See page 63 for audio script.

Speaking

7
Model conversation

Jun	So I'm coming to visit you and other people next month. What topics should we discuss?
You	*First, we can discuss the project schedule.*
Jun	Good idea. What next?
You	*Second, we have to check the project costs.*
Jun	I agree. And after that?
You	*After that, we **need to** talk about the problems with the consultants.*
Jun	Yes, that is a big problem. Anything else?
You	*Finally, we **have to** go out for dinner.*
Jun	That's a very good idea!

Unit 15 Dealing with questions in the conference call

Telephone conference call

Diane suggests a conference for the senior management level of Lowis and APU. At first John is not sure about the suggestion but in the end he thinks it is a good idea.

See page 64 for audio script.

Understanding

2

1 B   2 C   3 C

Practice

3

1 D   2 A   3 B   4 C

4

1 I'm sorry but could you repeat that last word?
2 What do you mean by 'delayed'?
3 But I don't understand why it's a problem.
4 Can you give me an example of this?

5

1 I'm afraid I don't / is it
2 you give an
3 there a reason why
4 I'm / Could you repeat
5 But I don't / what

6

See page 67 for audio script.

Speaking

7

Model conversation

Supplier	Then there was a strike at the factory.
You	*I'm sorry. Could you repeat that?*
Supplier	There was a strike.
You	*I'm afraid I don't understand the word.*
Supplier	Oh, I see. A strike. The workers stopped working.
You	*Oh, I understand now. Is there a reason why they had a strike now?*
Supplier	Well, they weren't happy with the new terms and conditions.
You	*Can you give me an example?*
Supplier	Well, first the workers wanted more money.
You	*Can you repeat that? I'm afraid I didn't hear what you said?*
Supplier	The workers wanted more money.

Unit 16   Written invitations

Email

1 The conference will be in London on January 10. Joe Smith is not sure at the moment if he can attend. He needs to change his plans.

Understanding

2

1 False, the email is sent to senior managers at APU and Lowis.

2 True

3 False, Diane and John want people to email them with their answer.

4 False, the information about the conference will be sent when they answer the email.

5 True

6 False, Joe is not sure at the moment.

Practice

3

1 We are pleased **to** invite you to the opening of our new offices in Penang.

2 We would be grateful **if** you inform us about you plans.

3 We **look** forward to welcoming you to our new offices in the near future.

4 This occasion **will** be an opportunity to meet senior managers.

4

1 dade. date

2 plaice place

3 next near

4 Truly truly

5

1 We are pleased to invite you to our sales conference on September 13.

2 The event will take place in the Tower Hotel.

3 The occasion will be an opportunity for you to meet our staff.

4 Yours truly

Writing

6

Model email

Dear Colleagues

We are pleased to invite you to the opening of our Munich factory. The event will take place on April 4 at 10.00 am. This occasion will be an opportunity to see our new equipment in action.

We would be grateful if you could reply before March 1. As soon as we receive your reply, we will send details of the event, the location and the hotel.

We look forward to meeting you at our factory opening.

Yours truly

James Scott

7

Model email

Dear James

Thank you very much for your invitation to the opening of the Munich factory.

At the moment I'm not sure if I can be there. As soon as I know, I will get back to you to say if I can attend.

With thanks

Unit 17   Business trip details

Email

1   Pia is writing to Tom to give him information about his hotel in Sydney and other arrangements.

Understanding

2

1   The hotel will send a limousine to meet Tom.
2   Pia wants Tom to send flight details.
3   Tom can check the hotel facilities on the hotel's website.
4   John is taking Tom to the opera house to see *Carmen*.

Practice

3

1   B   2   E   3   A   4   C   5   D

4

1   Jasmine will arrange for the documents to be photocopied.
2   I would like to confirm your landing time at Singapore Airport.
3   You can find more details in the attached document.
4   Let me introduce myself – my name's Jasmine Goodman.
5   Please call me if you have any problems.

5

1   ~~my~~ me
2   ~~will~~ would
3   ~~four~~ for
4   ~~are~~ is
5   ~~detail~~ detailed
6   ~~cheque~~ check
7   ~~has~~ have

Writing

6

Model email

Dear Ms Binders

Let me introduce myself – I am ....'s assistant, and **I would like to confirm** your hotel arrangements.

I have booked you into the Harunami Hotel for three nights (March 23-26). The hotel has sent me a confirmation code for your reservation, HH23MAR211.

For further information about the hotel, **please check their website** here: **www.harunami_hotel.com**

... has reserved a table in a restaurant for March 24. She / He will meet you in the hotel lobby at 7.00 pm.

Please contact me if you have any questions.

Yours sincerely

XYZ

Unit 18   Changes to the schedule

Email

1 Tom is staying for eight days in Australia.

See page 76 for audio script.

Understanding

2

1 Tom Field – Lowis Engineering
2 Wants to change ~~hotel~~ *schedule*
3 Arrive Sydney Oct 16
4 Hire car Oct 19
5 ~~Visited Sydney already~~ *Hasn't visited Sydney already*
6 Send ~~letter~~ confirming details *email*

Practice

3

1 D   2 C   3 B   4 A   5 E

4

1 can
2 ask
3 Would
4 kind
5 lot

5

Jasmine	Jasmine Goodman, Lowis Engineering London. How can I help you?
Eva	Hello. This is Eva Schmidt here. I wonder if I could ask you a favour.
Jasmine	Of course, Ms Schmidt. What can I do for you?

Eva	Well, you booked me a room at the Tower Hotel for three nights. Would you mind changing the reservation to only one night? For the last two nights I'm going to stay with friends.
Jasmine	No problem. So you only want a room for October 31st?
Eva	That's right.
Jasmine	Fine. Would you like me to organize for you to be met at the airport when you arrive?
Eva	No, it's OK, thank you. I'll take the underground. But thanks a lot for your help with the arrangements.
Jasmine	My pleasure!

Speaking

6

See page 79 for audio script.

7

Model email

Frank	Frank Richards speaking
You	*Hello, it's Jim Levy here. I wonder if I could ask you a favour.*
Frank	Of course. What can I do for you?
You	*I wanted to ask if you could change my meeting time with Mr Ho.*
Frank	I'm sure we can find a time. When is convenient?
You	*Would ten o'clock on Tuesday be possible?*
Frank	Let me see … well, I need to change another appointment of Mr Ho's, but that's not a problem.
You	*Oh, that's great. Thanks a lot for your help with the arrangements!*
Frank	My pleasure!

Answer key / Audio script

Unit 19 Welcome back to the office

Video
1 Tom didn't like the stop at Moscow.

See page 80 for video script.

Understanding

2

1 C   **2** A   **3** A

Practice

3

1 It's nice / good
2 What was
3 Did you do
4 Good to see
5 What did you
6 It's nice / good to have you back.

4

1 What did you get up to in Paris?
2 What was the weather like when you were in Seattle?
3 Did she do any sightseeing when she was there?
4 Is everything going well in Shanghai?
5 Good to see you again!

5

Robert	Hi, Jasmine. Good to see you again!
Jasmine	Hello, Robert. Nice to have you back! Good flight?
Robert	No, it was awful. But Beijing was great!
Jasmine	Really? Did you do any sightseeing?
Robert	Some. I saw the Great Wall.
Jasmine	Fantastic! What was the weather like?
Robert	Oh, great. On the hottest day it was about 35 degrees!
Jasmine	Lucky you. It rained here.
Robert	Yes, Diane told me. But still, it's nice to be back!

Speaking

6

See page 83 for audio script.

7

Model conversation

Cathy	Hello! Good to see you again.
You	*Hi, Cathy! It's nice to have you back again. Did you have a good flight?*
Cathy	Yes, it was fine.
You	*Is everything OK in the New York office?*
Cathy	Yes. I had a very interesting time.
You	*Did you do any sightseeing?*
Cathy	No, not really. But I did go shopping.
You	*Lucky you! What did you buy?*
Cathy	Well, I went to Bloomingdale's because I've always wanted to go there. I bought a bag.
You	*Great! What was the weather like?*
Cathy	Oh, it was good. Sunny and warm.
You	*It was very cold here.*
Cathy	Oh, dear.

Unit 20   The project review

Video

1 The integration of the accounting systems is behind schedule.

See page 84 for video script.

Understanding

2

1 False, John and Karen are worried about the project. They think it's going too slow.

2 True

3 True

4 False, no, they aren't. Not yet.

5 True

Practice

3

1 E   **2** C   **3** A   **4** B   **5** D

4

Suggested answers

1 Can you show me the figures for July?

2 I don't understand why it takes so long.

3 When did you speak to him?

4 Have you written the email yet?

5 When will you finish the job?

5

Suggested answers

1 Let's look at the project schedule.

2 Here we can see the problems with the costs.

3 Moving on to the question of quality.

4 The next slide shows the next steps.

Speaking

6

See page 87 for audio script.

7

Model conversation

Team member	So let's look at the project status then. Here we can see the costs so far.
You	*Can you show me the time schedule?*
Team member	Yes, well the next slide shows the detailed schedule for the system integration and the training programme.
You	*Have you started the training programme yet?*
Team member	No, we haven't started it yet.
You	*I don't understand why not.*
Team member	Well, the equipment isn't ready yet.
You	*When will it be ready?*
Team member	It'll be ready by the end of this week. But we've finished the software update already.
You	*Good! When did you do that?*
Team member	That was on Friday last week.

Unit 21   Starting the video conference

Video

1   No, they can't solve the problem.

See page 88 for video script.

Understanding

2

1   Karen and John have a problem.
2   They can't make their video conferencing equipment work.
3   They call a technician.

Practice

3

1   keep
2   click
3   wrong
4   on
5   trouble

4

1   We're having trouble with the server.
2   I think we need to call the help desk.
3   Just a moment, please.
4   When I open my email account, my computer crashes.
5   The telephone doesn't seem to be working.

5

1   My system has crashed.
2   I'm having problems opening my email account.
3   There seems to be something wrong with the printer.
4   The internet doesn't seem to be working.
5   Sorry to keep you waiting.

Speaking

6

See page 91 for audio script.

7

Model conversation

Help desk	How can I help you?
You	*There seems to be something wrong with my computer.*
Help desk	OK. What's the matter?
You	*I seem to be having problems with the screen.*
Help desk	OK. Have you tried to reboot your computer?
You	*When I click on the restart icon, nothing happens.*
Help desk	Have you tried to turn off the computer and then restart?
You	*Hold on a moment.*
Help desk	No problem.
You	*Sorry to keep you waiting. No, I think I need a technician.*
Help desk	OK, I'll come up to your office.
You	*Thanks a lot.*

Unit 22 Discussing problems in the video conference

Video

1 Diane doesn't want to put pressure on the accounting department.

See page 92 for video script.

Understanding

2

1 False, Karen and John think the integration of the accounting department is going badly.
2 True
3 False, Diane disagrees with Karen.
4 False, the accounting team doesn't have enough people.
5 True

Practice

3

1 B 2 D 3 E 4 A 5 C

4

1 sure
2 sorry
3 not
4 absolutely
5 so

5

Fiona	We need to open a new office in Moscow for our Russian customers. What do you think?
Simon	Yes, I agree. We need to be close to our customers.
Tom	Yes, but at the moment we don't have any customers there, do we?
Simon	I don't agree. We have some business with Vladivoil. We need to increase that.
Fiona	I think so too. Russia is the next big market.
Tom	I'm sorry but I don't think it's a good idea. It's vey expensive to open an office in Russia.
Simon	We need to remember the costs. You're quite right. Perhaps we should close the office in Sydney and then open an office in Moscow.
Fiona	I'm sorry but I don't think that's a good idea, Simon!

Speaking

6

See page 94 for audio script.

7

Model conversation

Dale	Well, the next point on the agenda is IT strategy. We need to decide what to do next about our business management system.
You	*You're absolutely right.*
Dale	In the US we think we need to update our business management system.
You	*I'm sorry but I don't think that's a good idea. The present system works fine.*
Dale	But the new system is really easy to use!
You	*Well, I don't agree. I think the new system has problems.*
Dale	Well, the present system does work well.
You	*I think so, too.*
Dale	But the new system is much faster.
You	*Look, let's continue the discussion at lunch.*
Dale	Good idea!

Unit 23   Finding solutions in the video conference

Video

1 Diane suggests that APU send people to help the Accounting department at Lowis with the system integration.

See page 96 for video script.

Understanding

2

1 C   2 A   3 B   4 C

Practice

3

1 C   2 A   3 E   4 B   5 D

4

1 How about hiring a new trainer?
2 We could always ask him if it's important.
3 Why don't you arrange another meeting?
4 What can we do about the situation?
5 What about changing our computer systems?

5

Tom	So, Robert, what can we do about the IT integration problem?
Robert	What if we ask APU if we can do the integration next year?
Tom	No, APU says it must be this year. What else can we do?
Robert	We could always hire some extra people.
Tom	That's too expensive. How about asking people at APU to help?
Robert	Good idea!
Tom	Can you give me a list of the people you need?
Robert	Of course. If this doesn't work, I'll lose my job!

Speaking

6

See page 99 for audio script.

7

Model conversation

Angie	Well, we need to decide what to do about the English training next year. What do you think we can do?
You	*How about sending people to the UK or Australia?*
Angie	I think that's too expensive.
You	*Well, why don't we hire an English teacher?*
Angie	But it's difficult to know if they are good English teachers.
You	*We could always work together with a good school.*
Angie	Yes, that's a good idea. What should I do next?
You	*What about checking how many people want to study English?*
Angie	Good idea!

Unit 24   Ending the video conference

Video

1   Their next video conference is the same time Thursday next week.

See page 100 for video script.

Understanding

2

- *John will ask for accounting specialists to fly to London.*
- ~~*Diane*~~ *Karen will look for IT specialists.*
- ~~*Karen*~~ *Jasmine will arrange hotels and security passes for team.*
- *I will set up videoconference for* ~~*Tuesday*~~ *Thursday next week.*

Practice

3

1   her
2   suit
3   think
4   When
5   covered
6   See

4

1   Does Monday afternoon next week suit you?
2   Let me check my schedule for next month.
3   That time's good for us.
4   So to recap our discussions today.
5   When is a good time for Mr Holden?

5

1   So let me recap, ...
2   I think that covers everything.
3   When should we next meet?
4   Let me check my schedule.
5   Does Tuesday suit you?
6   That's good for me!

Speaking

6

See page 104 for audio script.

7

Model conversation

Tony	Well, have we covered everything?
You	*Yes, I think that covers everything.*
Tony	So to recap, my team must be trained to use the new system. And the trainers can be provided by this company, xSoft. Is that correct?
You	*Yes, that's right. When should we have our next meeting?*
Tony	Let me check my schedule.
You	*Does Tuesday at four o'clock suit you?*
Tony	Sorry, no. How about two o'clock?
You	*That's good for me.*
Tony	Great. Shall we go for a coffee? I need one!
You	*Me too. Good idea.*

Answer key – grammar reference and practice

Exercise 1

1 work   2 is focusing   3 is helping
4 arrives   5 is staying   6 is not feeling

Exercise 2

1 Diane is visiting the APU offices next
month. 2 Aren't you going to the party on
Saturday?   3 I'm afraid we're visiting my
mother this weekend.   4 She isn't arriving
until Tuesday.   5 They're meeting the
President at three o'clock.   6 Is he flying to
LA soon?

Exercise 3

1 do / come   2 come   3 do / work
4 work   5 does / arrive   6 gets
7 does / go   8 takes

Exercise 4

1 I'm   2 going   3 Is   4 to   5 Isn't

Exercise 5

1 finished   2 didn't speak   3 Did / telephone
4 did / do   5 didn't email   6 had

Exercise 6

1 E   2 A   3 F   4 C   5 B   6 D

Exercise 7

1 on   2 in   3 at   4 in   5 on   6 at

Exercise 8

1 much   2 many   3 a few   4 many
5 a little   6 much

Exercise 9

1 have to   2 must   3 have to   4 mustn't
5 have to   6 don't have to

Exercise 10

1 harder   2 better   3 more cheaper
4 worse   5 happier   6 more difficult

Exercise 11

1 the biggest   2 the worst   3 the
best   4 the fastest   5 the most
suitable   6 the most expensive

Exercise 12

1 C   2 E   3 A   4 B   5 D

Exercise 13

1 can / can't   2 able   3 couldn't
4 Can   5 can't   6 be

Exercise 14

1 C   2 E   3 A   4 F   5 B   6 D

Exercise 15

1 is   2 soon   3 finished   4 until   5 wait

Exercise 16

1 Have you ever been to New York?   2 She
hasn't signed the contract.   3 We've moved
offices again.   4 The company has won the
Sunstone contract.   5 I've already finished
the report and sent it to my boss.   6 Has he
answered your email yet?

Exercise 17

1 B   2 D   3 A   4 C   5 F   6 E

Exercise 18

1 quickly   2 slowly   3 early
4 suddenly   5 fast   6 intelligently

Exercise 19

1 The conference was cancelled last week.
2 The package will be sent by courier.
3 Her reports are read by the top
management.   4 The temperature is
checked every five minutes.   5 I must be
driven to the airport.   6 The house is heated
with solar power.